To
Luke Sun

Best wishes

2/93

THE ENTREPRENEUR'S SURVIVAL GUIDE

101 Tips for Managing in Good Times & Bad

THE ENTREPRENEUR'S SURVIVAL GUIDE

101 Tips for Managing in Good Times & Bad

John J. Cullinane

BUSINESS ONE IRWIN
Homewood, Illinois 60430

This publication is designed to provide accurate and authoritative information in regard to the subject matter covered. It is sold with the understanding that neither the author nor the publisher is engaged in rendering legal, accounting, or other professional service. If legal advice or other expert assistance is required, the services of a competent professional person should be sought.

From a Declaration of Principles jointly adopted by a Committee of the American Bar Association and a Committee of Publishers.

Sponsoring editor: Cynthia A. Zigmund
Project editor: Susan Trentacosti
Production manager: Mary Jo Parke
Jacket designer: Michael Finkelman
Printer: Book Press, Inc.

Library of Congress Cataloging-in-Publication Data

Cullinane, John J.
    The entrepreneur's survival guide : 101 tips for managing in good times & bad / John J. Cullinane.
      p.   cm.
    Includes index.
    ISBN 1-55623-823-1
    1. Industrial management. I. Title.
HD31.C823 1993   92-23891

Printed in the United States of America

2 3 4 5 6 7 8 9 0 BP 9 8 7 6 5 4 3 2

To

Diddy, John and Sue,

Mrs. Haverty and My Family

About the Author

In 1982, 1984 and 1985, John Cullinane was named as *The Wall Street Transcript*'s CEO of the Year in the computer software products industry. Mr. Cullinane has been inducted into the Babson College Academy of Distinguished Entrepreneurs and was honored in 1985 at the Fifty-Seventh Annual Awards Dinner of the National Conference of Christians and Jews. Most recently, he was inducted into INFOMART's Information Processing Hall of Fame.

Mr. Cullinane was Founding Chairman of the Board of Directors of the John F. Kennedy Library Foundation and the Massachusetts Computer Software Council. He is also a member of the Board of Directors of Sentry Publishing, Inc., Blue Cross/Blue Shield of Massachusetts and the ADAPSO Foundation.

Mr. Cullinane was graduated from Northeastern University, and its Alumni Association presented him with the Northeastern University Outstanding Alumni Award for Business and Industry. He has also received honorary degrees from the University of Massachusetts, Boston and the University of Lowell.

During the past year, John Cullinane was a Fellow in the Center for Business and Government, John F. Kennedy School of Government at Harvard University, where he authored a paper on the short-term focus of American corporations entitled, "Widows and Orphans." He also organized a series of seminars for CEOs, including "The CLT Petition — Good or Bad for Massachusetts?" and "The Credit Crunch," which focused on credit problems impacting New England banks, real estate developers and other businesses. He also hosted a conference on telecommunications sponsored by Governor Weld of Massachusetts and Congressman Edward Markey.

Preface

Cullinane Corporation (the Company) was the prototype of all high-fliers to come in the computer software products industry. After a rocky beginning in 1968, the Company compiled a record 13 years of uninterrupted annual growth of 50% or greater in both sales and profits, including 29 quarters of such performance as a publicly held corporation and a five-year stretch of having the highest price/earnings ratio on the New York Stock Exchange (57:1). It also became the first software company to attain a valuation of $1 billion.

Such a performance couldn't go on forever. Inevitably, there was going to be a "down" quarter, and that is what eventually happened. But as Bruce Springsteen would say, "Time slips away and leaves you with nothing, Mister, except boring stories of glory days." [ASCAP84]

This book presents some of what I learned from the Company's founding to its eventual sale -- lessons that could be of benefit to the reader in founding, building and sustaining a business in good times and bad. While much of it is in anecdotal form, a major effort has been made to reduce the complexities of these corporate experiences to simple messages or essays that may be useful to other executives who find themselves in similar situations. In some ways, it is my "expert" system in that much of the knowledge I have regarding running an organization has been reduced to these pages.

[ASCAP84] ©1984. Bruce Springsteen. ASCAP.

Acknowledgments

I wish to thank Martha Cummings, my administrative assistant, who "word-processed" so many versions with a remarkably good nature. Colleen Frye's editing suggestions were most helpful, as were the suggestions of Ed Bride, John Desmond and Mike Bucken and the editorial staff of *Software Magazine*. Special thanks also go to Rita Arthur and, in particular, to Lillian Larijani, my editor, and Cynthia Zigmund, Senior Editor at Business One/Irwin, for their help and advice.

John J. Cullinane

* *Throughout the book, profiles are provided for persons whose names are marked by asterisks.*

Contents

THE ENTREPRENEUR'S SURVIVAL GUIDE

101 Tips for Managing in Good Times & Bad

Introduction

In 1954, as a Northeastern University co-op student assigned to Arthur D. Little, Inc., Boston, I witnessed the installation of one of the first commercial computers, a Burroughs 205. At that time, people had great expectations for computers — expectations that still prevail today. When the Burroughs machine was installed, the company's chief financial officer said that everyone wouldn't be fired immediately; they just wouldn't be replaced when they left.

But it was a long time before computers performed anywhere near the claims of vendors, particularly in the business world. This was due to a very simple fact: Computers were developed in university environments to solve complex equations, particularly during World War II, and were, as the name implies, well designed to do *scientific computing* but very poorly designed to do business data processing or information handling.

In the early days, the programmer would manually enter a limited amount of data, plus a set of instructions representing the formulas, into the computer and then watch the lights of the "electronic brain" blink while the computer solved the equations. The answer might appear as one line of printout after minutes or hours of computing, depending on the complexity of the problem. Since businesses do mostly data processing and very little computing, this was just the opposite of what any company required.

The power of computers in the information systems environment is used primarily for housekeeping tasks — namely, maintaining billions of items of data being accessed and updated by, in many cases, thousands of users. Very little computing, relatively speaking, is performed in a typical business application.

The challenge, therefore, was to re-engineer the computer into a data processing and communication machine. This has taken place on a significant scale only in recent years, and it required much more than hardware. It required an investment in software for data processing, data communications and user interaction — all while the cost dynamics of computers was changing remarkably fast.

These economies have had dramatic impact on hardware and software vendors in recent years. However, one of the laws of computing is that small, simple computers invariably grow to become powerful, complex, multi-user computers. One negative is that multi-user software is exponentially more difficult to develop than single-user software. Personal computer users and manufacturers are now finding out how true this is as they develop software to support personal computers that are evolving into end-user workstations that are, in turn, becoming part of a network supporting many users. The "little" computers have all the technical problems of the big computers.

Nevertheless, it is now possible to store, update, manipulate and retrieve data from large databases of information located anywhere in the world via networks linking mainframes, departmental and end-user workstations and personal computers. As standards emerge to help remove unnatural communications barriers between hardware and software, the movement to global networks incorporating many vendors' platforms is happening at an astonishing speed. A pervasive influence of computers is now taking place in our society, far more so than predicted in some of the most hyperbolic press of the 1950s and 1960s.

Key to this success has been the evolution of software, the coded sets of instructions necessary to make a computer perform its tasks. Yet, for many years, software was considered a nuisance, something that would eventually fade away to be replaced by some magical mode of communication that would eliminate the need to communicate with an idiot in a dead language. One of the reasons for this attitude is that, historically, hardware manufacturers were in the "iron" business; they sold "boxes," the more the better. Speed of the machines was paramount; the fact that a user couldn't do anything with the computer didn't faze the vendors.

A typical attitude, as recent as the late '60s, was that of a highly respected computer industry guru, who told me, "There is no future in computer software. Hardware is the only way to go." Since the Company was formed to specialize in computer software products and was struggling at the time to survive, this wasn't a very encouraging piece of advice. I was often told that it couldn't be done. Others had tried and failed; so would I.

Fortunately, the analyst couldn't have been more wrong. Software couldn't be replaced so easily, and people who had formed software companies – in particular, packaged software companies – began to sell enough products to make money and to do better than just survive. Most of these companies specialized in mainframe software, including business applications and systems software, because that was where the market was.

Some things haven't changed

in almost 50 years.

Regardless, software has always been incredibly difficult to develop. For example, there is an anecdote included in the book, *Brighter Than A Thousand Suns* [Jungk58], which chronicles the Manhattan Project and the creation of the Atomic Bomb. Robert Oppenheimer, the project leader, was complaining to John Von Neumann, the great mathematician and inventor of the MANIAC computer, that the lack of vital computations was holding up the project. He wanted to know what was causing the problem. Von Neumann's answer was, "The programming is taking longer than they estimated."

What's unique about this response is that it took place in 1944 and is probably the first known recording of the infamous phrase still uttered throughout the software industry. Nothing has changed in the almost 50 intervening years! Just scan some news releases from famous software companies, and you'll see that this phenomenon continues to occur today.

[Jungk58]   Robert Jungk, *Brighter Than A Thousand Suns*, Harcourt Brace, New York, 1958.

Chapter One

Managing the Entrepreneurial Urge

CONFIDENCE

I learned that from experience comes confidence. For example, when I was first promoted to a managerial position, I was asked to go to Washington and meet with both the executive management of my corporation and my contemporaries. At the time, this company, a forerunner of all computer services companies, was in difficult financial straits. As a very young, novice manager, I went to Washington with great trepidation, naively expecting to find brilliant management housed in a tower that somehow enabled them to communicate with God over important decisions. After sitting in the meeting for just few hours, it dawned on me why the company was in trouble. Management didn't seem to understand the business or have solutions to its problems.

After this exposure, I no longer felt out of my league and was sure that common sense could be applied to a much greater extent in solving my region's problems. I returned to Boston eager to try imaginative, new ways to build the business. As a result, within one year, our center went from losing $50,000 per month to making $50,000 per month.

It is critically important to continually put yourself into situations where you can grow and gain confidence in yourself and in your ideas. I know this to be true because, like so many people, I had so little confidence starting out. It is the one factor that differentiates so many people, regardless of their actual capability, and the best confidence comes from experience.

Confidence is the "X" factor.

Entrepreneurs might also keep in mind that intelligence and verbal skills are a powerful duo but not necessarily related. Perhaps you've noticed how some people quite impressively articulate and sell questionable or dumb ideas. Well, it's often only their confidence that convinces. If you lack that edge of confidence to lobby your ideas convincingly, you undermine your effectiveness.

Force yourself into new situations. You may learn that you are just as good or better than many of your contemporaries.

BOBBY ORR

I first met ex-Boston Bruins star Bobby Orr while playing in the Greater Boston Business for Charity Pro-Am Golf Tournament at the Weston Country Club. Just as I was about to hit a shot, I noticed a gallery of one following our fivesome. It was Bobby Orr, of all people. I was startled that Bobby Orr, after all my years of watching him do great things on the ice, was actually watching me do something that was not at all great. Why was he following our team in the first place?

Naturally, I dubbed my shot but decided to say hello to him and tell him that, while I was very pleased to meet him, I was puzzled as to why he was following our team. He confided that one of the people in our group, Ralph Dacey, was a fellow member of his club, had recently lost his wife and was very down about it. Bobby was following us for a few holes just to cheer him up. My reaction was, "What a nice thing to do, so typical of what I had heard about Bobby Orr."

About that same time, I had an opening on the Company's Board of Directors and had been thinking about different candidates. I had not found a perfect fit yet as each of the potential candidates duplicated, to one degree or another, the talents we already had on the Board. I thought, "Why not Bobby Orr?" He was gracious to people, regardless of the impositions that might be placed on him by some of those people.

I checked with Jim Cotter, a mutual friend. He reported that Bobby was smart and quite savvy from a business point of view. I met with him, was impressed and asked him to join the Board. Everyone was delighted just to meet him. However, the question remained whether he was going to be just an adornment or a real contributor to the Company.

Bobby turned out to be intensely interested in doing a good job for the Company and attended week-long training classes on the Company's products and strategies. He also attended User Weeks and worked hard meeting with clients and prospects, all of whom were delighted to meet him.

Bobby Orr is "the Natural."

On one airplane trip, the on-board movie was "The Natural," which featured Robert Redford portraying a larger-than-life baseball player. As I watched the film, I thought, "No one could be that much better than his fellow players." It then occurred to me that I was sitting beside "The Natural" of hockey. Intrigued by the thought, I took a peek at Bobby. He was watching the movie intently. I wondered what he was thinking but somehow felt it would have been inappropriate to ask.

Sometime after Bobby joined the Board, an article by Frank Deford appeared in *Sports Illustrated*. [Deford85] When Frank asked Bobby if he had ever been nervous before a hockey game, Bobby said no, not even before the Stanley Cup finals, but he did say the most nervous he had ever been was just before his first Board meeting at Cullinet Software!

We soon learned that Bobby Orr had great insight. In short order, he became one of the most astute observers of the Company's scene. No one asked more penetrating questions or gave me better advice than Bobby. He's as natural in business as he is on the ice. However, I do think being on the Board of the Company helped Bobby's confidence in that he could stand out in a sophisticated group of high-tech executives just as he did everywhere else. I know it wasn't easy for him at first, but he made the effort. The transition from being a famous athlete to competing in the business world is much more difficult than you might think. Few have made it because few have tried as hard as Bobby.

If Bobby Orr can gain confidence via a new experience, so can you. He didn't have to join our Board of Directors, but he took a chance, and it worked out well.

[Deford85]   Frank Deford, "Hello Again, Old Friends,"
Sports Illustrated, August 5, 1985.

THE OPPORTUNITY INDUSTRY

The beauty of the computer industry – in particular the software segment – is that it provided so much opportunity for so many of us. The technology was so complex that if you could do the job or, better still, knew how to make something work, nobody cared what you looked like or what your family tree was.

> *America is still*
>
> *the land of opportunity.*

As a result, the industry has broken down many of the ethnic and social barriers that have dominated American businesses. The industry's willingness to tap the energy of the most capable people in America, regardless of background or gender, has made the American computer industry the most powerful competitor in the global economy. In the past, too many traditional American companies and industries have discriminated, to their great current detriment. But in the software industry, all you needed was an idea, the courage to launch a new company and, hopefully, the ability to bring it to life – as so many have done during the past 40 years or more. So many people have benefited as a result, it would be impossible to determine the true impact.

However, it is good to stop and recognize that history shows that economic happenings like the computer industry are very rare, indeed, and being in America made it possible for many of us to take advantage of the opportunity. For this I thank my parents, who had the courage and foresight to come to America from Ireland even though it must have been difficult for them to leave such a beautiful land. In essence, they were the ultimate entrepreneurs.

ENTREPRENEURS

Most people come to this country to find a better job. If there were any hope of economic improvement in their country of origin, they would be very reluctant to leave. All anybody wants, including our own disadvantaged, is a job. Unfortunately, because of the economy, a lot of Americans, including their sons and daughters, are finding out what it is like to be without a job and with no good prospects for finding one.

That's why being an entrepreneur is such a noble profession. A successful entrepreneur creates jobs. In an era when almost all large companies are downsizing, new jobs have to be created, and entrepreneurs seem to be doing a better job of it than anyone else. Peter Lynch of Magellan Fund fame is always quick to point out that, in the 1980s, the 500 largest firms in the U.S. eliminated one million jobs. During the same period, other companies, many of them entrepreneurial ventures, created 18 million jobs. In addition, when an entrepreneur creates a company, that company, in turn, creates additional jobs in the services sector. Most of the large office buildings in our cities are filled with law firms, advertising agencies, accounting firms, real estate firms, and so on, that are providing services to companies located elsewhere, and many of these weren't in business as recently as ten years ago.

That's why, when people contact me as part of their "networking" efforts to locate a new job, I suggest that they think about becoming an entrepreneur. After all, whenever I meet someone from high-school days, "someone who knew me when," I ask them what they are doing. Invariably they say that they have formed their own company, and it's doing well. When I ask them what prompted them to go out on their own, the answer is usually, "I figured, if you could do it, so could I."

And so can you.

Being an entrepreneur

is a noble profession.

My agent questioned this. She said I was making it sound too easy. Her experience as an entrepreneur for four years was that it was very difficult. She was always worrying about the business, sometimes booked only one month out and disliked selling. Earl Tate, an owner of a minority business, also recently complained to me about how difficult it was to generate new business in this economy. Well, it isn't easy, but it's worth trying. Welcome to the club.

SALES

My first assignment, after participating in the New England Telephone & Telegraph's highly competitive management training program, was as Business Office Representative in three Greater Boston communities. At the time, the State Police and an honest and courageous Assistant District Attorney, John Irwin (now a judge), were conducting an aggressive campaign against gambling operations in those communities.

The result was that I spent six months in court, giving testimony regarding telephone company records. The two things I learned while in court were that there seemed to be no rich people there, only poor, and that, to be convicted, one had to be guilty of breaking a specific law, such as using a telephone for gaming purposes. After six months of this duty, in the interests of my well-being, I was assigned to a new position in sales.

After a while, it occurred to me that, if I were in sales, I might as well get paid for it. So, when I saw an advertisement in the paper for a sales trainee at a computer services firm, I debated whether to respond to it. I didn't envision myself as a salesman. My image of salespeople was not good. Yet, salesmen seemed to be on the front lines making things happen.

Finally, after wrestling with the idea for a few days, I called the company, and a meeting was set up with George White, the sales manager. He offered me a job on the spot but said he was sorry that he could only offer me a job as a sales trainee, beginning at $7,500 a year. This was so much more than I was making that, with much trepidation, I decided to accept the offer.

> *If you want to be an entrepreneur,*
>
> *learn how to sell.*

A few weeks after I joined the company, George White said that Tuesdays were going to be "prospecting" days. I asked a senior salesperson what that meant. He said that you go out and make "cold" calls on companies — just walk in to a receptionist and ask for someone. I was stunned. I hadn't planned on that and had to force myself to do it. I can still remember sitting in my car outside some building or plant, getting up the courage to go in and hating it every time.

Yet, there was great personal satisfaction when business eventually came from some of these efforts. Within six months, I was given a territory including a number of accounts. Within another six months, I was making three times the amount I had been making at New England Telephone & Telegraph only 12 months earlier. With base salary checks, commission checks and expense account checks, money seemed to be coming in all the time.

Also, I was learning so much about computer-based technology, such as CPM, PERT, linear programming, time-series analysis, mathematical modeling, etc., and how this technology could be applied to certain business problems that it was very exciting. Whenever I brought our top technical talent together with the heads of research of various organizations, I would get an inside look at these companies' most critical problems and how computers could be used to solve them.

Computers were so new that we were doing missionary work. Best of all, I was free to go wherever I wanted, when I wanted, and I rather liked the competitive aspects related to sales performance measurements. Within another six months, George White was promoted to the New York office. He, in turn, promoted me to run the Boston office even though I was the youngest and least experienced person in the group.

Going into sales was a huge risk for me. I didn't think I was well suited for it at all. In fact, I took a sales aptitude test just out of college, and results said that I wasn't. I had real problems with questions such as, "If you are helping your grandmother across the street and a truck suddenly bears down on her while, at the same moment, you notice a $5 bill on the street, would you pull your grandmother out of the path of the truck or go for the $5 bill?"

Since then, I have learned that all people in responsible positions, particularly entrepreneurs, have to "sell" in order to promote their companies, products, services or ideas, and very few know how to do it well. From presidents of companies to president of prestigious universities, all have to sell to succeed. The sales training and related experience that I had garnered from this job were to serve me well in the future and leave me with a lasting impression of how tough it is being a salesman on the front lines. As a result, I have always tried to provide the Company's salespeople with all the support and advantages possible.

TAKING RISKS

When any new opportunity presents itself, ask yourself this question, "A year from now, by pursuing this opportunity versus staying where I am, assuming a worse-case scenario in both situations, such as getting laid off, will I be more valuable in the job market after the experience gained in the new job than I would be by staying where I am?" If you will be able to get a new job more easily after a year with the new venture or opportunity rather than by staying in the old job, then it's a "no brainer." Therefore, the risk is more a state of mind than a reality.

> *Risk is often a state of mind.*

The real obstacle to risk-taking is that most individuals hate to change a comfortable situation for the unknown. It's easy to fall into the trap of "retiring" on the job. I've seen it happen many times, and you have to force yourself out of it. Then you will most likely look back and say, "I'm glad I did it. It was easy, once I made the decision." At the very least, you owe it to your family to enhance your value in the job market.

AN IDEA

I first had the idea for a software products company in the 1960s, when I was Vice President of Marketing for a traditional custom-programming company. The company's business was to design and implement "one-of-a-kind" software for customers, using a wide range of computers. One contract required the company to build a generalized payroll system for a Rhode Island bank. Our company overran the contract.

Soon, we received another contract for twice the amount to build a similar generalized payroll system for a Connecticut bank. The company overran this contract, as well. Eventually, we received a contract from a bank in Buffalo for, again, twice the amount of the previous contract. As you might guess, the company overran this contract, too. Just as the development team was finishing this system, a New Jersey bank asked us to build a generalized payroll system for their computer system, which happened to be identical to the Buffalo bank's computer configuration, a GE 415, six-tape system.

At that point, the thought occurred to me, "Why don't we just sell them the system that we are in the process of completing?" In other words, we would be treating software, for the first time, as a product.

We sold the New Jersey bank the Buffalo bank's system for $20,000, and they were running payrolls within two weeks with a far superior system than they had originally envisioned. We accomplished this with 10 man-days' effort on our part as opposed to the man-years of effort required to develop a new system − with all its attendant testing problems, etc. The bank also paid the invoice right away. This made a big impact on me. This was the way to do business!

Recognizing the obvious before

anyone else makes you a pioneer.

Today, selling software as a product might not seem like a particularly imaginative idea, but in 1964 it was. In those days, most companies had a "not-invented-here" syndrome. They believed in building all systems in-house. To do otherwise was a negative reflection on their technical skills.

Nevertheless, it was obvious to me that the advantages of buying proven software off the shelf were overwhelming when compared to developing custom software. Most importantly, it was an idea that I kept in the back of my mind while I tried to gain the much needed experience and confidence to form a company of my own.

GETTING PUSHED OVER THE LINE

After two and a half years with this software firm, I had helped build the company into a very successful organization but was in the mood for a new job. Though I had been unhappy at the company from the very beginning, I had stuck it out because I did not want to look like a "job jumper." Eventually, I was offered the opportunity to open a Boston office for a high-level consulting firm. The firm specialized in database management technology, product planning and systems engineering, all of which were new activities for me.

Thus, the move to a consulting firm had its risks, not the least of which was walking away from my old company, an issue not as simple as it might seem. I had a major equity position (5%) in that company, and I would be giving up an opportunity for great wealth if I left for the new job. Anyone who left the old company had to sell his or her stock back to the firm at book value. In my case, it was $13,000. A few years later, the company sold out to Wang Laboratories, and many people became millionaires, as I would have, had I stayed. However, I so disliked the job that my wife and I felt the money wasn't worth it.

There was an additional risk associated with this new job because consulting services are extremely difficult to sell and deliver. In fact, the Boston office of the consulting firm was budgeted to lose $20,000 during the first six months of operation. Through a combination of luck and hard work, we made a $20,000 profit instead, a swing of $40,000, and I was selected for the firm's "Outstanding Performance Award" that year.

Good employees are often driven away

for the silliest of reasons.

As I mused about how large the award would be — $10,000? $5,000? $2,000? — I kept reducing the amount of the bonus because the management of the company, while otherwise very good, was a little on the tight side. Eventually, the president of the company flew to Boston to give me my award. He shook my hand and told me how pleased he was that I had been selected for the Outstanding Performance Award. He said the award was for $500; then, after a pause, "payable over three years." He also told me I would have no vested rights if I left the company prior to three years.

Well, my first thought was, "It's time to form that packaged-software company I've been thinking about."

While that might have been a good company, and they were nice people, there was no financial future in it for me, regardless of what I might do; the president owned about 99 per cent of the equity. I was another productive employee driven away for a silly reason. With a little more generosity I, and many other employees, might still be there, and the company might still be in business. In fact, I had now witnessed a number of companies where management seemed to drive employees away. Why couldn't a company be good at marketing, management *and* technical development? No company that I had been associated with in the past seemed to do all these things well.

THE LETTERHEAD TEST

The idea for packaged software had to be tested. I used an inexpensive but effective market research effort to determine the answer.

> *The best way to test your idea*
>
> *is to ask someone to buy it.*

Specifically, I made appointments with potential buyers I knew well at major corporations. I explained the concept of packaged software and asked them, "Would you buy software products and related services if they were available?" As friends, they were naturally positive in their comments. However, to really qualify them, I asked them to issue me a nonbinding letter of intent, written on their corporate stationery, stating that they would be interested in buying software products from my company if, and when, they became available.

Getting corporate executives to issue a letter of intent on their corporate stationery was the test. Most executives, regardless of how friendly, were nervous about using their corporate name and position in such a way. It forced them to think about the idea and whether they would really consider buying software products. To me, this was testing the marketplace in the most effective way available to me – and at no cost.

These letters were included as part of my financial proposal, and they were most influential in convincing the investment banking firm to help underwrite the Company. If you can't get an obvious prospect to do at least this much, then maybe it isn't such a good idea. Maybe it's time to go back and find another idea. Incidentally, ideas are easy to come by. Bringing them to life is incredibly difficult.

PARTNERS & OTHER MISTAKES

One mistake made by many entrepreneurs when forming a company is that they give away too much equity in the beginning in order to get commitments from management-level candidates. They usually do this so they will have an impressive management team in the company business plan.

Friends and relatives

don't mix with business.

It's not necessary. When it comes to bringing people into your new company, it will be far less expensive, from an equity point of view, if you form your company first, raise money and then get a nice suite in an upscale office park.

If you negotiate with someone in your family room on a Sunday afternoon, trying to get him or her to give up their job on the speculation that your new enterprise will get off the ground, it will be a very expensive proposition for you. What might cost you as much as 10%, 20% or 30% in equity before the fact may cost you only 1% after the fact. An additional irony is that, if the company does become successful, some of these same individuals' value may not keep pace. You will end up with large pieces of corporate equity in the hands of people who are no longer contributing to the success of the company.

And the same rule of thumb about not borrowing money from friends and family has a subclause: Don't go into business with friends and family either. It invariably leads to trouble. If you value your relationships with these people, don't test them by including them in your new business.

TEMPTATION

Right in the middle of forming my Company, I received a call from a major New England bank holding company that is now called Fleet Financial, Inc. A data-processing firm that they had purchased, with the help of a consulting firm under their new one-bank holding company status, was in trouble. Apparently, the president of the newly acquired firm took his money and quit, and they were looking for someone to take his place. They offered me the job.

There will always be good reasons

not to form your own company.

I clearly remember the dilemma I faced as I drove up Route 95 from Providence, Rhode Island. I had just been offered a seemingly fantastic job as president of a major computer services company. Should I take it or pursue the highly risky route of a new venture?

Two things were obvious to me. One was that the bank subsidiary had a lot of problems. The other was that the senior management of the bank didn't appreciate how significant the problems were and how difficult they would be to rectify. If I did a great job, it probably wouldn't be appreciated. When I compared this situation with starting a company with a clean slate and no existing problems, I decided on the new company approach.

The offer to become an instant president versus the unknowns of the new venture was, admittedly, very tempting. In retrospect, though, the instant presidency would have been a big mistake. In other words, there will always be a reason *not* to form your company.

START-UP CAPITAL

In starting a new company, it's important to follow some good advice I received from a variety of sources. The first maxim is: Don't put everything you own at risk in the new company. You're taking enough chances without also risking the security that you and your family might have by, for example, mortgaging your house. Also, be very reluctant about asking friends and relatives for money. If things go wrong, and they usually do, they probably won't have additional funds to invest in your company, and your relationship with them will suffer greatly.

> *Ask for twice as much money*
>
> *as you think you will need*
>
> *because you will need it.*

Most importantly, you should ask the investment banker or venture capitalist for twice as much as you think you will need because you will need it. In fact, many investment people would rather do a bigger deal than a smaller one. Quite simply, investment bankers make more money on a bigger deal than on a small one. This isn't true of venture capitalists; however, they do like bigger deals these days because they have so much money to invest. So, don't be shy about asking for money. If successful, you'll make millions for them.

Finally, be very tight-fisted with the money that you do obtain because it will disappear much faster than you ever dreamed possible.

MANAGING THE ENTREPRENEURIAL PHASE

1.   Force yourself into new job situations because from experience comes confidence.

2.   Test your idea *before* you go into business, not after.

3.   Good ideas are easy to find. Bringing them to life is extremely difficult.

4.   Don't go into business with friends and relatives.

5.   Don't give away the equity store to attract management.

6.   By all means, if you have had success at other companies, start your own company.

7.   Don't be afraid to fail. In fact, assume you may fail. It's not the end of the world if you do. In fact, you may be able to get a better job because of the experience gained in forming your own company.

Chapter Two

Managing the Start-Up Phase

INVESTMENT BANKERS

In my quest for financing the new venture, I called an old friend, *George White, who thought the idea of packaged software was a good one and recommended Laurence Fordham, a local lawyer, to help me form the Company. He also identified some people at a New York investment banking house for me to see for financing.

However, when I met with Laurence, he asked, "Why go to Wall Street? I know some Boston investment bankers. You should talk to them first. I'll set up an appointment." I was skeptical because of the extreme conservatism of many Boston investment bankers of that era (1960s). I should note that this conservatism is no longer the case. Besides, there are a lot of venture capitalists around now, which was not true in 1968.

We visited an old-line Boston investment banking firm and met the managing partner in his huge office. He was so interested that he arranged a follow-up meeting with his assistant. When we arrived, we found that the assistant's office was located in a renovated coat closet so small that he had only half a desk and just one chair. Since he had two visitors, one of us had to stand.

It so happened that the bank was making another deal at the time, and he said they couldn't help us. It struck me as comic and ironic to be standing in this investment banker's little closet office while he sat behind half a desk discussing such large sums of equity capital. Then he surprised us by asking us to be paid consultants on the spot to review the other deal. It was a computer timesharing company whose business plan had, in our opinion, some very large holes. For example, the computer they were going to use could support only thirty-two terminals concurrently, versus the sixty-four terminals the company was including in their financial proposal. When we pointed out this major flaw, the investment banking firm thanked us for our work and said they were glad that we had found no "major" problems in the proposal. They did the deal, much to their later regret. By this time, we were in negotiations with a New York firm.

> *Money to new ventures flows more easily in some cities than in others.*

A former business associate and friend of George White's, *Sol Manber, opened the door for me with Ted Rosen at Burnham & Company, a New York investment banking firm. The firm agreed to raise $480,000 for 40% of the equity in the Company, purely on the idea of packaged software that the Company would acquire from corporations not in the software business and then repackage, sell and support. The fact that they had made a lot of money on some of Sol Manber's ventures helped our cause greatly.

Within approximately six months, the investment company had raised the $480,000. On the day of the close, however, a $24,000 investor dropped out, and Sol, already a participant, agreed to pick it up rather than have the deal collapse. In his opinion, it was the best investment he has ever made.

Working with those partners at the investment banking firm who worked for Ted Rosen was a most unusual experience. During the negotiations, we would often go to Oscar's, the Wall

Street high-roller restaurant of the time. It would be filled with Wall Street operators discussing their deals. During our first lunch, I was startled to hear one of the partners uttering religious expressions reminiscent of my Irish Catholic mother, such as "Thanks be to God," or "Jesus, Mary and Joseph," or "God Willing." I certainly hadn't expected to hear such expressions in those so-called halls of greed. The partner made the statements with the fervor of a monk; only in his case it had to do purely with making money. I soon learned that he was a former Christian Brother and teacher before getting a job as an analyst on Wall Street. Such are the career paths of many Wall Streeters.

Now they were doing deals as investment bankers and becoming very successful, so successful that some people believed they had the "magic" or, as Tom Wolfe described Sherman McCoy, a bond trader on Wall Street in the novel, *Bonfire of the Vanities* [Wolfe87], they were "masters of the universe." As a result of their success, many doors were opened to the partners, including some very conservative Boston investment houses. The last time I saw them, they were forming the investment banking arm of an over-the-counter house and looking at corporate jets to help them make bigger deals, faster. However, the market conditions turned very bad very fast in 1970 and, as often happens on Wall Street, there never was any jet nor an investment banking arm of the brokerage house. Eventually, there was no brokerage house and no jobs. Nonetheless, Howard Goldberg and John Matkovich were two good guys.

> *Getting the money is only the beginning.*

When our deal closed, I flew back to Boston with checks amounting to $480,000 in my brief case. When I got home, I laid the checks out on the dining room table. Frankly, they didn't look like very much, just a bunch of personal checks. What had I done? Could a successful business be made out of packaged software? I didn't know, but the reality of what I had done began to set in. I knew I was going to have to deliver in the very near future. At that moment I felt very uneasy.

Of course, by the time the bankers and the lawyers had taken their cut, there was a big chunk gone out of that $480,000, and I hadn't even gotten started.   However, the impression that was particularly lasting was that, if any group required government regulation, it was Wall Street.   The events of the '80s and '90s have only confirmed what happens when it isn't there.

George White: George was my first boss in the computer software and services business and also gave me my first promotion, a position I was astounded to even be considered for, let alone receive.   I always admired George for this because, at the time, I was the youngest and least experienced person in the group, and it would have been very easy for him to give the job to someone else.   George was also the one who suggested I speak to Sol Manber about my idea.

Sol Manber: Sol is a wonderful and generous person, an ordinary seaman in World War II who was eventually graduated from M.I.T.   He holds many patents and knows more about law than most lawyers and more about finances than most accountants.   One of his companies, Alphanumeric, Inc., was so successful initially that any venture he was interested in was welcomed by Ted Rosen at Burnham & Company.

[Wolfe87]   Tom Wolfe, *Bonfire of the Vanities*, Farrar, Straus & Giroux Inc., New York, 1987.

WHY REINVENT THE SOFTWARE WHEEL?

In November 1968, the Company got under way in an old building in downtown Boston with approximately 10 employees.   The Company's original purpose was to acquire the products from companies that used computers but were not in the software business, such as banks.   The initial products acquired included an installment loan system, proof of deposit and a cost estimating system.   The most aggressive thing that we did was commit to a full-page advertisement in *The Wall Street Journal*, which cost $30,000, an enormous amount of money at the time and almost 10% of our cash reserves.   The headline of the ad was,

"Why Re-Invent The Software Wheel?" It generated about $30,000 worth of consulting business — enough to pay for the ad — and caused a lot of people to wonder who Cullinane Corporation was.

Once we acquired the software products, selling them turned out to be extremely difficult because they were applications, which require a longer selling cycle. The major reason we had difficulties, however, was because the products were not state-of-the-art systems. Being number two in a software evaluation process is like being number two in a poker hand. It's emotionally very unsatisfactory and also very expensive.

> *New ventures rarely go*
>
> *according to plan.*

Consequently, the cash reserves were diminishing at an alarming rate. We needed to change horses in mid-stream and develop our own software.

*Gil Curtis, our key technical person at the time, mentioned that the Company had developed a product in-house to facilitate installation of applications — in essence, a program library update system. It made it easy to install the applications and send updates at a later date. Since most companies at the time maintained their programs in card-deck form in file cabinets, there was a tremendous need for such a system. We decided to promote this product under the name of Plus-Sequential.

The Company engaged in a telemarketing effort and created a considerable interest in such a product. There was only one problem: The product was a sequential (tape) version when the market wanted a direct access (disk) version. While we sold some copies of Plus-Sequential, we helped create a terrific market for Pansophic Software, Inc., whose first product was Pan-Valet, a direct access system. By the time this became obvious, our very modest technical resources were working on our second non-application product, the Culprit Report Generator, and we wouldn't be able to develop a direct access version until it was too late. Yet, the revenue generated from these products was helpful in keeping the Company going while Culprit was being created by *Ann Marie Thron and Gil Curtis.

Gil Curtis: Gil and I became acquainted at Phillip Hankins & Company, Inc. (Arlington, Massachusetts), later acquired by Wang Laboratories, Inc. Its software expertise was the key to Wang's early great success. I ran into Gil in an airport, and he said to me, "If you ever do anything on your own, let me know. I'd like to do it with you," and I thought, if a good technician like Gil felt this way, maybe I could form a company. It was an important chance meeting. Gil is now Vice President of Programart Corporation (Cambridge, Mass.).

Ann Marie Thron: Ann Marie, an outstanding programmer, was the major developer of the Culprit system. She would never lift her head from her coding work all day. Gil and Ann Marie eventually formed their own company called Programart Corporation, which developed the STROBE product. Ann Marie recently retired as Vice President of Development.

OUR FIRST CRISIS

When the Cullinane Corporation was about two years old, it faced its first major crisis. Quite simply, we were running out of money. We were going bankrupt. This was taking place even though we had done everything possible to generate revenue by providing consulting services and marketing other companies' programs to conserve our cash position.

The situation deteriorated to the day where we had only $500 of the original $480,000 investment left and a payroll of $8,500 due that day. Fortunately, a check for $8,500 arrived in the mail that morning, just in time to meet the payroll.

The problem was that our one product, a report generator package called Culprit, wasn't selling very well. In reality, we had no money, no technical resources and no time left. It was what I call a problem!

We sold fewer copies of Culprit than we had projected because the product lacked basic capabilities. For example, Culprit prospects wanted a good file-matching capability, which Culprit didn't have. We tried to convince the prospects that they were wrong and that they should write their own file-matching routines, which most didn't know how to do. The result was that, while many Culprit prospects thought Culprit was a terrific product and a major technical advancement, they eventually bought inferior technical products from competitors because their products had the file-matching capabilities.

There is always a crisis.

I had to cut the staff from nine people to five, reduce office space from 5,200 square feet to 1,500 and stretch accounts payable, etc., to survive. I was convinced we would be bankrupt in six months. The two remaining technicians, *Jim Baker and *Jeanne LaPointe, tried to be responsive to customers' needs, as our customers perceived them. For example, within six months, Jeanne had built file-matching capabilities into Culprit. Things then took a change for the better. Key to turning the corner was the "EDP Auditor" version of Culprit.

Jim Baker: A graduate of M.I.T. and a Ph.D. candidate at Harvard University, Jim, at the lowest point in the Company, came into my office and said, "If you're worrying about me bailing out, don't because I am with you all the way." Since he had six kids, it was a courageous and most appreciated statement. Every program Jim wrote worked perfectly. Jim is retired and lives in Harvard Square, Blue Hill, Maine and London, England.

Jeanne LaPointe: Jeanne, the son of French-Canadian immigrants, had taken a programming course while a business machine repairman. Within six months, he was able to build a file-matching capability into Culprit. He also became a Vice President and received a salary equal to Jim Baker's – at Jim's suggestion. Jeanne left one day after he had purchased land down south, and I have not heard anything of him since.

RAISING MONEY: PART II

Despite our best efforts, in 1971 we were still going broke. Consequently, I made another visit to Wall Street with Board members George White and Sol Manber. Sol took us to meet with Ted Rosen, who was then President of Black Securities. One problem at that time was that investment banking houses were folding faster than you could follow through with appointments with them.

When we arrived at Ted's office, he was on the telephone and signalled us to come into his office. We couldn't help but overhear his conversation with his caller, and what we heard got us very concerned.

The person at the other end of the line was obviously selling Ted Rosen hard without success, and the caller had quite an argument. The company that he wanted Ted to invest in had been in business over 100 years and had made money every single year since its inception. It turned out to be Luchow's Restaurant, a former well-known German restaurant.

Sometimes you are going to have to find a solution other than money.

What a record! However, what was disillusioning was that Ted wasn't buying. What could we say when he finally hung up on the caller and turned to us and asked, "What can I do for you?" Our Company had been in business only three years and had lost money all three years. We thanked him very much for his time and withdrew as gracefully as we could.

It was obvious there wasn't going to be any second-round financing for the Company. We were just going to have to work our way out of our troubles or perish, but how?

LOAVES AND FISHES

I was aware that a few customers were using our Culprit package for EDP auditing purposes. But what did an EDP audit software package do? I didn't know, but I found a copy of a publication listing a "Big 8" accounting firm's requirements for EDP audit software. Comparing these requirements with Culprit's capabilities, I found there was a remarkable match and was very pleasantly surprised that Culprit was actually a major advancement over a typical EDP audit package from a "Big 8" accounting firm. Our product was fast, more powerful, could access any file, including database management systems, and produce any report, regardless of complexity. However, a major drawback was that Culprit was designed for use by programmers, and most auditors had little EDP background.

It's much easier to develop

new markets for an existing product

than most CEOs realize.

The solution was to create a new version of Culprit called EDP Auditor. While Culprit and its spin-off were actually the same system, for EDP Auditors we provided a considerably different level of support and training, which was tailored to non-programmers. For example, we were the first to form an EDP Auditors' Users Group. Each user spoke about how they were using the product – of great value to the other attendees. We also programmed an EDP Auditor Library of commonly used routines, such as audit verification notices and statistical sampling, to go with the product. As a result, we were making the auditor's job easier.

Everything that we offered gave these professional auditors something they wanted. In particular, our technical support gave them the independence from the data processing department they so desired. The result was something very important to auditors, namely, the "integrity of the audit."

The first customer to buy the EDP Auditor System was a bank that had already purchased the Culprit system. They recognized the value of the services we provided and were willing to pay additional for them. Sales improved immediately, and we survived.

Developing the EDP Auditor system was what an employee called "the parable of the loaves and fishes."

THE UNANTICIPATED RESULT

As auditing departments used the new EDP Auditor package, the fast turnaround of reports quickly caught the eye of senior financial management. Data processing departments had traditionally given three-month estimates to all types of end-user requests for reports in order to either get rid of end users or discourage them from asking for more reports. The auditors were producing quite valuable and impressive reports in days, and management began asking, "How could this be when the data processing department said it would take three months?" and, "Why can't data processing produce reports like these?" As a result, data processing departments, long resistant to products like Culprit because their programmers would have had to have changed their ways of doing things, began buying the package as a defensive move.

Incidentally, this need by users to circumvent total reliance on data processing departments is one of the underlying reasons for the eventual great success of personal computers and software such as report generators, query languages and relational database management systems. In order to get their jobs done, management and others had to find ways to access and analyze corporate data directly.

So, what we couldn't sell well at $10,000 (Culprit), we were now selling a lot of at $20,000 (EDP Auditor/Culprit). We had identified a special market niche and responded to it well. We had also hired our first sales person who could sell software. His name was *Jim Blake.

As we coped with our early crisis, we also learned something very important about organizations. When our money was running out, and we cut back from nine employees to five, there was a concern that our service would suffer. The unanticipated result, to my great surprise, was that we accomplished much more with five people than we had with nine. This was because these five employees clearly understood that we were in business to satisfy our customers' needs and because the interaction and communication among them were extremely effective.

> *A few people pulling together*
>
> *can accomplish great things.*

We were pulling together with a common mission. It still amazes me how much can be accomplished in this type of atmosphere. One of the benefits of this teamwork included becoming profitable for the first time in the Company's history.

Jim Blake: I found Jim Blake's initial interview fascinating. Everything I threw at him, he calmly hit in a logical and convincing manner. Jim always delivered on what he promised and proved that a good salesman could sell any system. He was very smart and had been an honors graduate of Boston College.

MAKING MONEY

Making money is the ultimate challenge for any entrepreneur. It requires great self discipline. It also helps to be an imaginative fundamentalist who quickly determines that the secret to the success of your new venture is in one or two key areas of the company. In the case of our Company, it was in sales. If I could figure out how to sell software as a product, there was great potential for profits. To date, no one had solved that problem. People said it couldn't be done; others had tried and failed. Consequently, that was where I spent most of my time.

If the key to success had been in creating the software, I would have concentrated on that. I don't think the Company would have survived if I had spread my time equally over the three activities of finance, development and marketing. Consequently, I gave a lot of responsibility to our technical people.

The shorthand methods I developed for estimating and controlling costs used to frustrate the financial people because they were so simple, yet could be so accurate. The cost aspects were simple, determined by how many employees the Company had.

The imaginative part of cost control comes in when you try to figure how to reach some goal without spending any money. It may include the sharing of facilities at a trade show or a computer center, or it could include a joint development effort with a client or prospect interested in a new product – both forms of barter that save on badly needed cash. Successful entrepreneurs, out of necessity, get very good at this.

Volume does not equal profits.

Finally, great self discipline is required to make money because only you stand between your corporate treasury and all those who wish to take it from you. Often, your staff will demand equipment or services to do their jobs better and view you as the unreasonable or uncaring person standing in the way. Your salespeople, on the premise that volume equals profits, will want you to sign contracts with clauses that could cost you money down the road.

Thus, making money in any new venture is not easy. While every venture I have been associated with has made money, and lots of it, it was always a constant battle. In any successful entrepreneurial venture, there is usually only one person with his or her eye on the bottom line – you.

SPECIALIZATION

The surest route to success for any new venture is through specialization. It takes courage because there is a great temptation for a start-up company to be all things to all people and to solicit business from any source. The problem is that, after a few years, you may have difficulty in differentiating your company from any other, assuming that you are still in business.

The easier you make it for a potential customer to recognize what is unique about your product or service, the better it will be for your business. For example, let's say you drive a BMW that badly needs a tune-up, and you pass three garages on the way to work, all of which have expert mechanics. The first displays a sign, "Mechanics on Duty." Chances are you will not stop. If the sign at the next garage reads, "Mechanics on Duty, Specialists in Foreign Cars," you will be considerably more interested. However, if at a third garage the sign reads, "Mechanics on Duty, Specialists in BMW Cars," then chances are that you will stop and inquire about their service. Think about all the potential customers who "pass" your company every day because they don't understand why they should do business with you.

Specialize.

Be an expert at something.

When I formed the Company, I remember Jim Davis, a Vice President of Marine Midland Bank in Buffalo, stressing the importance of specialization. If you followed the Company, you would find the word "specialists" prominent in our promotional efforts throughout its history. The Company specialized in audit software and database management systems at different times and actually used related themes on its letterhead and in its advertising. At one time, in fact, all Company advertisements carried the message DATABASE:CULLINANE in large type at the bottom of each ad. It would prove to be very effective in associating the name of a new company with leadership in the evolving field of database software.

An unusual example of specialization, the "Moishe Peking" Kosher Chinese restaurant in New York, was introduced to me by Henry Weiss, Vice President of Montifiore Hospital. Even my Jewish friends found this hard to believe. I don't know how many Kosher Chinese restaurants there are in the world, but this one was always crowded, a tribute to specialization.

Another friend, Jack Cadagan, began his career just out of college representing a valve and fitting company. His company's products solved many of the unique flow problems found in research laboratories across New England. The result is that he has built a thriving business that has prospered in good times and bad.

In each of the above examples, whenever a prospect had a particular need, he or she was able to match a specific company with the need. It's your job to make it easy for them.

MANAGING THE START-UP PHASE

1. Ask for twice as much money as you think you will need because you will need it. Besides, it's much easier to get the necessary funding the first time than when you go back to the well the second time.

2. Hold on to your funds; don't waste them on fancy offices or facilities. Your funds will melt away so fast that it will make your head spin; so, don't burn them needlessly.

3. Don't use personal funds or put your family at risk financially by borrowing on your mortgage to underwrite your company.

4. There is always a crisis; business rarely runs according to plan.

5. There is no substitute for hard work. Your start-up will not be easy; no one said it would be. It takes time to build a successful business; so, make the calls.

6. Be imaginative when evaluating the strengths and weaknesses of your product or services. Build around your strengths; create a new product and/or market if necessary. Many successful companies change horses in mid-stream.

7. Continuously figure out ways to cut costs. Reduce your expenditures to those items that you must have to survive vs. those nice to have.

8. Make sure that you are selling a product or service to people or companies that have the money to buy.

9. There are advantages to being small. One of them is the ability to make decisions quickly and respond to a prospect's requirements on the spot. Your big competitors can't do this.

10. Specialize.

Chapter Three

Managing in Good Times

NEW OPPORTUNITIES (RISKS)

Late in 1972, there was a Presidents' Panel at The National Conference of the Association of Computing Machinery in Boston. On the panel was Al Jorgenson, who ran a timesharing company. A few months later, I ran into him on the shuttle to New York. He mentioned that he had recommended the Company to Jim Gilliam, a database administrator at B.F. Goodrich (Independence, Ohio), who was looking for a software company to take on marketing and support responsibilities for a database management system they called IDMS (for Integrated Database Management System).

I called Jim, even though the chance of our taking on someone else's program at this time was remote; we were turning down products all the time. He referred me to Dick Schubert, his boss, who in turn told me they had hired the consulting firm of McCaffery, Seligman and Von Simpson to help them make a selection. The firm had recently finished a study and recommended our EDP Auditor system to one of their other clients. So, obviously, they had to know us well; yet, I was astounded to learn they had not included us in the list of potential candidates. I called one of the partners, Naomi Seligman, and asked why we weren't included. She said, "You don't know anything about database management systems."

I responded that we did. I had worked with database management systems at a previous company, and some of our key technicians had valuable experience: *Tom Meurer worked with the Cincom Systems' TOTAL database management system, and Jim Baker had interfaced Culprit to IBM's IMS/DL1 system. She was impressed enough to at least include us in the study. Better still, after a number of visits to review our capabilities, she recommended the Company as the preferred vendor to B.F. Goodrich.

Now we had a very important decision to make. We had just become profitable after a very difficult start-up, and a database management system was a very complex product. There had been many horror stories about database management systems in the trade press at that time. Yet, to me, database was a foundation product around which we could build other products, including our report generator, Culprit. It would provide a long-term strategy for the Company.

It's important to have

a long-term product strategy.

Our technicians, in particular Tom Meurer, said IDMS was an excellent product when compared to the competition; so, I took a deep breath and said we would do it. I knew it was a "bet your company" decision. We signed an agreement in March 1973, but it would require about nine months to learn the system, properly document it and develop new versions of it before we could market it effectively. This meant that January 1, 1974 was the official launch date. As part of the contract with B.F. Goodrich, we had committed to sell 20 copies in the calendar year 1974. There were two major competitors at that time, Cincom Systems and IBM.

Cincom's TOTAL was a good but somewhat simpler product, for which the company had done an outstanding job of marketing. IBM, in turn, had a very powerful but complex system called IMS, which was expensive and difficult to use. So, we were stepping into a market where we were going to have to compete head-to-head with IBM and a very established independent. Most software companies were, and still are, afraid of competing head-to-head with IBM.

By late 1974 we had sold only five copies but still made our goal of 20 copies by the end of the year. We were lucky. IDMS turned out to be a superb product, and our philosophy of enhancing it to suit our customers' needs differentiated our product and services from competitors. In addition, IDMS was so stable that one of our customers, at Abbott Laboratories near Chicago, told me IDMS was "scary" because it would run for months without a bug or an error to bring it down.

For a 15-person company in 1973, it was an audacious move to take on IBM in database software. Since a customer, literally, ran his or her company with a database management system as the engine that drove the applications, it was a risky decision for any corporation. The sale of database management system to an IBM account was, and is, very important to IBM. They know that it means control of the account. For us it meant that every database sale was a battle with IBM and, since IMS was used primarily by big companies, a very small competitor had little chance. We also had no sales force to cope with IBM's thousands of representatives. I was always amazed that so many major companies bought this software from such a small company (at that time) as ours.

Tom Meurer: Tom is an extremely loyal and hard-working individual. His knowledge of corporate DBMS systems was key to our decision to get into database systems. Also, Tom was a source of many important ideas, as well as excellent at identifying and recruiting outstanding people.

TAKING ON IBM

With only 15 people, we had to maximize our resources in sales and marketing. Our solution was to conduct seminars around the country. This provided an opportunity to showcase our very small but outstanding technical staff by having them make the presentations.

There were always a few strong technicians in the audience who would become very intrigued with IDMS. One prospect included IDMS at the last minute in their database study, figuring that it couldn't hurt and could be eliminated quickly. Yet, the more they studied IDMS, the more they liked it and, in fact, finally had to recommend it over IBM's product.

We lost many situations like this, though, when IBM went in at a higher level and sold senior management with, "Do you want to trust the very life of your company to something called Cullinane Corporation, when IBM will always be with you? Don't let those technicians make another dumb decision." This is called "fear, uncertainty and doubt," or the "FUD" factor.

Nonetheless, being small, we were able to respond quickly to special customer requirements and to find enough courageous companies to grow 50 per cent a year. Yet, it seemed we were always in a battle of subjectives with IBM — "IDMS is easier to use, more powerful, etc." Senior management usually opted for a study, and the results were frequently close. I can remember one study that resulted in a 5,280-point total for IDMS and 5,260 points for IBM's product. A president or chief financial officer of a prospect would say to his or her MIS manager, "For 20 points, I should go with a company other than IBM? Are you crazy?" As a result, we lost a lot of business.

Being small is a bigger advantage

than most small companies realize.

A unique characteristic of the Company's sales approach was that almost every person we used in sales was a former systems programmer and an expert in database technology. This really impressed the prospects. Even when we didn't get the business, we developed a reputation of knowing more about database technology than any competitor.

Still, we had not really learned how to cope effectively with IBM, despite our successful growth.

LISTENING TO PROSPECTS & CUSTOMERS

Around 1975, the value of listening to customers and prospects became even more evident to me. People had begun to ask about data dictionaries. When I brought this up to our small, overworked technical group, they said they didn't have the time or resources to build a new data dictionary facility, and that was that.

So, how to get around this problem? The solution was a joint venture with a consulting firm that was very interested in developing a data dictionary. We agreed they would present a proposal to the IDMS User Group in Atlanta that fall to develop a data dictionary for any interested parties on a cost-sharing basis. When they presented the proposal, few companies wanted their dictionary approach, which was "inactive." Then we asked the question, "How many were interested in an *active* data dictionary?" All raised their hands. This unanimous expression of interest had a big impact on our development group, and we agreed to develop one.

> *If you don't listen*
>
> *to your customers' requirements,*
>
> *someone else will.*

An active data dictionary is a unifying product that drives all the components of a database management system. It is an extremely complex application, so complex that it caused us to make a most important decision. We decided to use IDMS as the database manager for it. Within six months, we had a test version of an active data dictionary, which we referred to as the Integrated Data Dictionary, and within another six months, we had installed the product at 20 sites. Within a year, our technical staff, including *Bill Casey, had turned an idea into a product that generated $200,000 worth of revenue, an incredible accomplishment.

The Integrated Data Dictionary, in the opinion of many industry observers, is still the most advanced data dictionary in the world and certainly the most complex application ever developed with IDMS. Frankly, we could never have developed the dictionary without the power of IDMS and its related tools.

The decision to build a data dictionary turned out to be a most important move by the Company. In fact, active data dictionaries are critical to new technology developments of the future, including distributed data processing. The key was that we listened to prospects and convinced our technical organization of the wisdom of building a data dictionary.

Bill Casey: Bill is a great wit and was intensely interested in all aspects of the Company. With Bob Goldman and Don Summers, he designed and developed the Dictionary and made enhancements to the product during its first installation at Boatmen's Bank in St. Louis. Bill now has a key technology job at *The Washington Post.*

CRISIS #2:   BIG BLUE STRIKES

The second great challenge to the survival of the Company came in its 10th year, just after we went public in 1978. This crisis taught us how really tough IBM can be, particularly when Big Blue turns its marketing force on you.

In January 1979, IBM introduced a new and very important computer called the IBM 4300 Series. Immediately, we started getting calls from very upset customers. It seems that IBM was telling our customers that the Company's database management system (IDMS) didn't run on this new IBM computer. Besides, all IBM applications of the future, according to IBM, would be based on IBM's competing database management system, IMS/DL1. In other words, our customers would be out of the mainstream of all future IBM application development.

IBM was selling this to senior management by telling them they had made a mistake in the past when they let their "technicians" acquire the Company's database management system.

Now it was time for management to correct this "error" and buy IBM's IMS/DL1. Every customer was very nervous and, worse, every prospect went on hold.

We had been public for only two quarters, and immediately we had the potential disaster of a down quarter on our hands if we didn't do something fast. The Company's vice president of technical development, *Bob Goldman, and I went to New Jersey to meet with a customer and a prospect to listen to their concerns first-hand.

One customer had questions regarding microcode, the new IBM 4300 and what would happen if IBM developed applications with IMS/DL1. This last item was of great importance to the customer. We answered the microcode question easily, and our technical staff, after making a small change, had IDMS running on the IBM 4300 computer in one day.

If customers and prospects

have problems with your company,

do something about it now.

In the car on the way over to the key prospect, Bob Goldman and I agreed we were going to have to develop an IMS/DL1 escape facility so that if IBM developed IMS/DL1 applications, they would run with IDMS. We decided on the spot to make a commitment to develop one. This made a very positive impact on the prospect and, eventually, all our customers. It relieved the FUD factor for these two companies. But we needed more than this to compete head-to-head with IBM.

At the end of the day, we were on a plane at Newark Airport, but it was delayed because Boston's Logan Airport was closed due to bad weather. I decided to rent a car and drive home, while Bob stayed on the plane. I was concentrating on the problem so intensely that, to this day, I don't remember the section of the drive from Newark, N.J. to New Haven, Conn., despite a terrible rain storm.

It eventually dawned on me that there was a clear differentiator between IBM's and our database products. Simply put, the components of our database management system were designed to work well together, and theirs weren't. It was because our database management system was driven by an "active" integrated data dictionary, and IBM's wasn't.

It was also obvious to me that we had to move our sales focus — from selling the technician to selling senior management. We decided to do this via a "management seminar" promoting IDMS as "the dictionary-driven database management system." Moving quickly, we invited our customers and best prospects to seminars held at our corporate headquarters for briefings.

The point of our products working together was an issue of fact and a major competitive advantage. IBM would have to acknowledge to prospects that theirs didn't, particularly if the Company made an issue of it, which we would eventually do. As a result, our credibility with management soared. Management liked the idea of putting IBM's "feet to the fire," as one prospect told me. They didn't often have the opportunity to do so.

The management seminars went very well because we got all of the tough questions up on the table and answered them forthrightly. We got through the fourth quarter successfully without a sales downturn and avoided a stock market catastrophe. In fact, we maintained our traditional growth in sales and profits.

However, it was a very close call. We survived only by moving very fast and effectively.

Bob Goldman: Quiet and mild-mannered, Bob had an ability to rise to any occasion. Often I would complain to Bob that we should be able to do something that he initially felt was impossible from a technical standpoint. The next morning, Bob would come into my office with a solution. Bob eventually became President of the Company and is now CEO of AICorp, Inc. (Waltham, Massachusetts).

SALES FORCES, THE HARDEST SELL

While the management seminars were an unqualified success, Bob Goldman, *Frank Chisholm and I were making most of these presentations at corporate headquarters or on the road. This wasn't good enough. We had to institutionalize it. Getting the staff to comply turned out to be the hard part. On a Wednesday flight to Toledo and back, Bob Goldman and I put together a presentation, slide by slide, featuring "IDMS, the Dictionary-Driven Database Management System." By the next Monday, our visual aids manager, Logan Smith, had it available and began making copies to distribute to our sales force. We were proud of our work. The crisis was solved — or so I thought.

We sent each regional manager a copy of the slide presentation and asked them to use it. This was something new for our regional managers, who were used to doing things their way. By chance, I followed up with some regional managers, such as *Flip Filipowski and *Ray Nawara, and found that they weren't using it — certainly not as it was intended. I couldn't believe it!

Sell the prospects,

and you'll sell the sales force.

Consequently, I sent out the only "Thou Shalt" memo in Company history, telling our salespeople to use the slide show "as is." To force the issue, we set up regional seminars for customers and prospects, and Bob Goldman and I conducted each seminar personally to make sure it was done the way we wanted. Most importantly, we wanted to demonstrate to our regional people how effective the presentations were. When our regional people saw the very positive reaction on the part of customers and prospects, they bought in quickly. This crisis taught us the importance of moving fast, the significance of product positioning, the need to differentiate the products and, most importantly, how hard it is to get a sales organization behind a new strategy, regardless of how good it may be.

Andrew "Flip" Filipowski: Flip and the other member of the dynamic duo, Ray Nawara, were incredibly bright and very hardworking. Flip could really sell. He is Founder and CEO of Platinum Technology, Inc. (Lombard, Illinois).

Ray Nawara: Ray was unusual in his capacity to listen and thereby improve his skills. He was extremely strong technically. Ray delivered on what he promised, and when he left to form DBMS, he turned over his region in great shape. Ray is now President of Cross Access, Inc., a software company.

Frank Chisholm: Frank, a great presenter and quick on his feet, was Senior Vice President of Marketing. I arranged to meet him at a presentation to McGraw-Hill after they had agreed on IBM's IMS. I brought with me the new slide presentation, which Frank had not yet seen. As each slide came up, he studied it and said exactly the right thing, resulting in a $220,000 sale. Frank is extremely personable and could "cut" a video tape in one taping session without having to redo any of it. He was on the Management Committee and is now President and Chief Operating Officer of AICorp (Waltham, Mass.).

CULLINET USER WEEK

In the early years, the IDMS User Association held annual meetings, which required about 300 people to sit in the same room for three days and listen to speakers, whether or not they were interested in what they had to say. This had to be very tedious for some users. An additional concern was how many of the attendees knew surprisingly little about our products, despite the fact that they may have participated in a training class at installation time. It was then that we created the concept of the Cullinet User Week, and the thought occurred to me, "Why not organize the User Week around education?"

The only drawback to running our own User Week based around training was that it might seriously hurt sales of our new Education Division. I took the chance that this might happen, but it seemed to me that sending attendees home from the User Week knowing more about our products was good for both the users and the Company in the long run.

Thus, all participants attended a morning class of their choice running from 9 a.m. until noon, Monday through Thursday. The only time all attendees were together was at lunch. In the afternoon, they attended special user presentations or product marketing presentations of their choice, and the Company's marketing presentations were clearly identified as such.

On Wednesday mornings, we conducted a special Executive Management Day for the senior management of our customers and prospects and presented to them where we thought the technology was going. We answered all questions from the floor and then asked customers about their plans and needs. As a result, we had a free, very valuable source of information on which to base future plans.

> *Doing what is best for customers always*
>
> *seems to produce unanticipated results.*

The Company also ran a business office during User Week so that members of the Company's management could meet with customers and prospects. The result was that we often sold 10 to 20 million dollars' worth of software at User Week. The reason is that prospects had spoken to users who were unanimously enthusiastic about the Company and its products.

An unanticipated result was that User Week was a big boost to our Education Division. Users would return home after taking a course they liked and recommend that others attend a similar course given by the Education Division.

The attendees would work incredibly hard, often from 7 a.m. to midnight or later. By Wednesday night, they were ready for a good time, and we provided it via a big banquet with entertainment, including Art Buchwald, Mark Russell and others. The users were so enthusiastic that they made a great audience. One year, they even sang "Happy Birthday" to a delighted Art. Another year, the crowd was so large that we came up with the idea to put an 80,000 sq. ft. tent across Boston's Copley Plaza with a 2500 sq. ft. dance floor to accommodate the Temptations and 4500 users. Diane Cramphin, who was in charge of User Week, was able to get the necessary 22 permits in two weeks, a remarkable accomplishment.

On Tuesday evening, the wind began to blow at gale force, almost blowing the tent down. Even worse, it was dislodging plate glass windows from the John Hancock Tower, crashing them onto the Plaza. Miraculously, at 6 p.m. on Wednesday evening, the wind died down, just in time for the show to go on. Otherwise, we would have had to cancel what turned out to be a fantastic show.

User Weeks were large, complex events with hundreds of concurrent sessions spread over multiple hotels, housing up to 5,000 attendees. Nothing was more important than User Week, and many were handled by capable employees that had been promoted from secretarial positions – including Rosalee Cope, *Martha Cummings, Judi Fahey, Elke Krajewski, Nancy Peterson and Marilyn Ricci. Diane Cramphin and Laureen Martel, too, did great jobs, as did everyone associated with User Week. It was always the event of the year, and the challenge was to top the previous year.

Martha Cummings: Martha was, and is, my assistant. One year, she was pressed into action at the last moment to take responsibility for User Week and did a fantastic job.

TECHNICAL DEVELOPMENT

The first program I ever wrote while attending an IBM programming class is a simple example of classic program development. I was assigned to a three-man team, and the final test was to create a program to solve an assigned problem. The other two members of the team were enamored with putting into the program all the "bells and whistles" they could think of. I was almost a non-participant in the effort. On the day of the test, I was sufficiently uneasy about their "comprehensive" program; so, I wrote another very simple one, just in case. Well, as you might have guessed, their program didn't run. At that critical moment, I handed my program to the computer operator, and it ran on the first try. The reason it did was because it was a very simple solution to the problem. It worked, and we didn't flunk the exam.

A more significant example is the Company's first effort in building an on-line query system for use with IDMS. The technical staff debated whether to develop the all-purpose natural language query system or something less. Developing a natural language query system might take five years and have significant performance problems, etc. My question was, "What could we develop in the shortest period of time that would do our users some good?"

The answer was that we could develop what was really an on-line display facility in three months. This display facility, which we called On Line Query Release 1, was enormously valuable to database administrators because it enabled them to look in the database to make sure it had been loaded properly. So, even though this first version was extremely limited in features and function, it did provide great value to at least one important constituency and generated considerable revenues in the short term, while relieving competitive pressures.

> *Technical decisions are often not*
> *technical but rather ones of judgment.*

Another variation of this theme was the Sequential Processing Facility (SPF) developed by *Ron McKinney. We had been losing many sales for lack of a sequential processing capability. Ron was in sales support and undertook to develop such a capability from his home terminal. While it wasn't a perfect solution, it filled a need and generated a lot of business.

It is worthwhile to note that when the Company had four programmers, we had twice as much work for them to do than they could possibly handle. When we had a 500-person technical staff, we also had twice as much work for them to do than they could possibly handle. As a result, I spent a lot of my time on prioritization.

What is interesting is how quickly the list of priorities changed. If a month passed between meetings when we reevaluated priorities, we would often find that we had valuable and scarce technical staff working on projects that were no longer on the priority list — and nobody working on the most important projects in the Company.

The most overlooked quality in the search for successful software development is good judgment. In fact, in software development most of the "technical" decisions aren't really technical; they are ones of judgment. Every case of late, bug-filled, poorly documented software has its origins in poor judgment. When a software project is in danger of being late, there is a remarkably simple cure for most of the problems. It has to do with the removal of features and functions.

Since most of the software products I have seen in the past 30 years are far richer than most users could ever possibly use, this approach is entirely practical. I have also found that a small group is ideal for developing software products. A team of four programmers with complementary expertise/skills plus someone to document their efforts seems to work best.

Ron McKinney: Ron is a most enthusiastic and supportive individual. He was totally committed to the customer and would go anywhere, any time, to solve a problem. He was willing to do anything to help the Company, and the Company helped him. Ron was a pleasure to work with, and his technical skill in solving problems was legendary. He is now an entrepreneur and founder of MAXSYS, Inc. (Akron, Ohio).

MANAGING IN GOOD TIMES

1.   **Introduce a new marketing strategy every two years.**

     Your customers, prospects and salespeople will appreciate it. This means your competitors' salespeople will be answering your questions. This is a sure sign that you're outselling the competition. However, the new strategy must be backed by good products, for which there is no substitute.

2.   **Have a major cost-cutting every two years.**

     In a growing company it takes two years for costs to get out of control. Therefore, it is imperative to cut costs, including a staff reduction, at least every two years. If you don't cut costs, regardless of how profitable the company is, costs will get away from you, and you will eventually need a major cutback. This creates all kinds of attendant problems.

3.   **Never invest in real estate.**

     Management of a growing software company invariably becomes enamored with real estate. There is a great temptation to build a corporate head-quarters located on a corporate "campus." The problem is that, while rapid corporate growth taxes management to the utmost, real estate is also a great consumer of management's time. Size of executives' offices, color of rugs, style of desks, floor layout and media capabilities of the executive conference room become major issues. A planned waterfall in the reception area is a sure sign that big trouble for your company is just around the corner.

MANAGING IN GOOD TIMES

4.   Find ways to get around the system.

Management by walking around is one way; personally meeting with customers and prospects is
another. It's imperative that you get around the "system" because the "system" will rarely give you the
right answer with the proper emotion. The bigger and
more successful you become, the more the "system"
(i.e., bureaucracy) takes over.

**5.   Understand that good references are key to
selling your products.**

Users are remarkably loyal to products they select and
that are supported well. If you give them good service, they will sell many copies without you realizing it.
Damaging this relationship with new versions or products that don't work or with unreasonable fees
should be avoided at all costs.

6.   Avoid investing in the "black hole."

Every successful company becomes so confident with
its success that it feels it has the "magic." Consequently, it finds some new venture to invest in that
allows it to pour the profits of their main business
down the "black hole" of expansion. No successful
company, regardless of size, is immune to this disease.

7.   Raise cash whenever you have the chance.

Raise cash when things are going well because something completely unanticipated will happen. Having
sufficient cash reserves will help you through the bad
times.

MANAGING IN GOOD TIMES

8.   Promote people with good judgment.

Most decisions in business are fairly obvious to a person with good judgment. In addition, most "technical" decisions are really ones of judgment. When it comes to promoting someone in your company, the most important question to ask is, "Which of the candidates has the best judgment?" The answer will invariably be, "So and so does, but..." The "but" will be followed by a variety of reasons why not to promote that individual. Always promote the individual with the best judgment.

9.   Invest in good information systems.

Many high-tech companies are like the cobbler's children. They don't understand the importance of practicing what they preach, namely, that "Information is Power." Knowing what is happening in your company in time to take corrective action is critical. For example, knowing which products you make money on and which you don't is a good start.

10.   Recognize that conducting business with integrity is not a burden but a great asset.

Many executives have discovered that conducting their businesses with integrity is one of the great secrets to success. It's much easier to do than most people realize, and it sure develops customer loyalty.

Chapter Four

Managing the Wall Street Experience

GOING PUBLIC

No amount of caution will cut through the "gold rush fever" that surrounds going public. It's the magic day for high-technology entrepreneurs. Many people become instant millionaires. The American Dream come true!

The Company, in 1978, was the first computer software firm to go public in 10 years. Consequently, there was great interest in the Company within the software industry. Its success, or failure, would impact other software companies that were waiting in the wings. In fact, the Company was the first software firm our underwriter (Hambrecht & Quist) took public, and going public turned out to be a very good thing for the investors and employees, all of whom had been given shares.

We were a "hot" stock. We came out over the counter at $20 and went to $28 on the first day. By 1985, the stock had split four times, and the Company was the first software company to attain a $1 billion valuation despite having sales of only $175 million. According to *Forbes Magazine* [Forbes], of all the companies that went public from 1975 to 1985, we had the highest appreciation. Even more impressive were the investments of $25,000 made in 1968. They generated returns of $25,000,000. No wonder the Company was viewed as the "darling" of Wall Street and represented the software industry so well.

In 1983, the Company was the first software products firm to be listed on The New York Stock Exchange. This stands out in my mind as one of those corporate/personal moments of accomplishment. To celebrate the occasion, we reserved a club car on a train to New York the day before the listing. We invited our Board members and Company executives and their spouses. It was great fun.

The ceremony the next day on the floor of the Exchange was also pretty impressive. The first trade of the day was reserved for the Company, as is the tradition for a new listing. A hundred shares of the Company's stock were purchased in London, and this trade and the name Cullinane were flashed around the world on all stock exchanges as the first trade of the day for The New York Stock Exchange. I was impressed and very pleased. Not bad for just an idea in 1968.

Going public is playing the

corporate game in the big leagues.

With a public offering, though, comes new and not very subtle changes in the management of the corporation. There is a myopia on quarterly results, with many attendant problems for American corporations in competition with Japanese and German corporations. For example, Japanese companies focus on customer satisfaction and market share. U.S. companies focus on earnings and return on investment. This is why customers of American publicly held companies are "orphans." "Widows" are unsophisticated investors who, for example, buy stock in a new venture on the day that it goes public at its high from the institutions who were included in the initial offering by the underwriter. As a Fellow at the Center for Business and Government at Harvard University, I have looked into this issue in a paper called "Widows and Orphans" [Cullinane91] because it is of great importance to any executive responsible for running a publicly held corporation. The following two chapters are excerpts from this paper.

[Forbes]   Richard Stern & Paul Bornstein, "Stacked Odds,"
Forbes Magazine, Forbes Magazine, Inc. New
York, July 14, 1986.

[Cullinane91] John Cullinane, "Widows and Orphans," The
Cullinane Group, Inc., Cambridge, 1991.

THE REALITIES OF QUARTERLY REPORTING

Each quarter after going public was a high-tension situation
while we "met the numbers." This is because there is no backlog
of orders in the software products business. Sales are usually
installed in the same quarter in which they are sold. We never
knew until literally the last minute of the quarter what the
revenues were going to be. Add to this the fact that the Company had the highest price/earnings ratio (57:1) on the New
York Stock Exchange for five years in a row – with an eventual
valuation of $1 billion – and you have the ingredients of ten-
sion. One slight slip could mean a one-day $500 million loss in
valuation.

> *To its great detriment, the American*
>
> *financial system does not encourage*
>
> *focus on the customer.*

In addition, the employees of new public companies are
often stockholders, and they, like others, begin to monitor the
performance of the company's stock on a daily basis. Sudden
moves up or down bring many questions from employees,
vendors, large stockholders such as institutions, as well as members of the company's Board of Directors. Many of these price
fluctuations may have little to do with the company's performance and are often due to selling by institutions such as
pension funds in attempts to make their own quarterly reports
look good.

Added to this are the tremendous pressures on management to perform in keeping with analysts' predictions. A great performance that doesn't quite meet analyst expectations is considered something of a failure.

In a publicly held company, the overwhelming need to produce good quarterly results shifts the focus from the customer to the bottom line. As much as 30 per cent to 50 per cent of executive management's time can be consumed in the reporting process, particularly as the quarter comes to a close; there isn't much time or energy left to focus on customer needs. Despite your best intentions, in this environment it is easy for your customers to become "orphans," a potentially deadly occurrence.

SO, WHY DID THE COMPANY GO PUBLIC?

Despite its drawbacks, a publicly held vehicle is a great incentive to entrepreneurs, as it was to me, and its job-creating value is of enormous value to the country.

There is no doubt that the pressures created by going public were counterproductive in an intellectual, product-development-oriented environment. Meeting quarterly and yearly financial goals is totally inconsistent with the nature of software development. Software products are rarely developed on time, within budget or completely free of errors. Trying to match this unique environment with the requirements of a quarterly reporting cycle is virtually impossible; yet, the Company did it without a hitch for 29 quarters in a row as a publicly held company.

But, in my opinion, it was like playing Russian roulette. Once we went public, the "fun" of the Company changed to pursuing the more shallow satisfaction of meeting quarterly goals and hoping the stock would increase in value.

The Company didn't go public because it needed the money. In fact, it was a "cash cow" that funded extensive new product development out of operating income while still maintaining 20 per cent to 22 per cent before-tax profit levels year in and year out. However, I never would have founded the Company, nor would investors have been available, nor would key employees have joined the Company, if we all didn't think that there was the possibility of a big payoff somewhere down the line, particularly from a public offering.

Getting rich is pretty exciting.

Any company with a track record to accommodate an IPO (Initial Public Offering) in a booming market is under tremendous pressure to do so. The window may be open for just a short period of time, and if a move is not made, years could pass before the next good opportunity arrives. In the Company's case, it had been almost 10 years since the last good "window." By late 1977, a member of the Board, Joe McNay, sensed that the window might open again in 1978. He guessed right.

When the Company went public on August 10, 1978, the stock market had one of its steepest climbs in a single day in the history of Wall Street. Therein lay the most important reason why we went public: Everybody had a chance to make a lot of money. No one in the Company was wealthy. This was their golden opportunity to amass some wealth. This certainly applied to me as well. Being so successful in our public offering and financial performance helped the Company generate business, as well. Chief financial officers and other members of a prospect's management team would often be aware of the Company's performance, and it would help sell products in competitive situations.

ROLE OF THE BOARD OF DIRECTORS

Boards of Directors are under extreme scrutiny these days from academics and others who specialize in corporate governance. There is a sense that Boards do not function well. However, one general statement I would make is that "outside" Boards are better than "inside" Boards. The reason is that many corporate problems are associated with existing management. Having these same members of management on the Board makes it difficult to discuss related issues when the Board meets.

Most Board members of major corporations do not have the time to adequately monitor or evaluate the professional management team's performance. They are usually incredibly busy people with their own company problems to think about. As a result, they have to rely on management, for better or worse. A company in trouble is a terrible burden to them. They also bear great legal responsibility for it.

Most Boards want to support management; consequently, they are inclined to vote for poison pills, golden parachutes and employment agreements. Why not? The average Board member is not a significant investor and has very little at stake. Compound this with the fact that individual investors have little corporate influence and that, because of regulation, institutional investors exercise very little power. This creates an atmosphere of absentee ownership, making it possible for even the best-intentioned professional managers to take advantage of a company. In addition, it is often very difficult to change management, even if performance is less than satisfactory.

No sane person should be on the Board of Directors of a publicly held company.

Professor William Sahlman of the Harvard Business School recently published and article in the *Harvard Business Review* entitled, "Why No Sane Person Should Serve on the Board of Publicly Held Corporations." [Sahlman90] His basic position is that the risks are great and the rewards are few. I agree. How would you like to have been on the Board of a failed bank or savings and loan institution?

Despite all of the above, I was able to attract some outstanding new people to the Board, including Thomas J. Flatley, President of the Flatley Company, J. Terrence Murray, Chairman of the Board, President & CEO of The Fleet Financial Group, Inc.,

Barry Rosenberg, General Partner, Cowen & Company and Gerard Doherty, an attorney. As a result, the Company did not want for a powerful and experienced Board of Directors.

However, a new phenomenon has arisen in recent years in the form of law firms that specialize in companies whose stocks are selling at high price/earnings ratios. These firms bet on the possibility that these companies may eventually have a "down" quarter. A few shares are purchased by a group of individuals known to the law firm. If the price of the stock tumbles on some unexpected bad news, the law firm then undertakes a class-action lawsuit on behalf of these few stockholders as plaintiffs against the company's executives and the Board of Directors. In addition, the law firm represents all stockholders who may have purchased or sold shares during a specific period of time. The aggregate amount sought may represent millions of dollars; yet, the firm's real clients may have lost only a few hundred. The law firm makes its money via the legal fees generated in representing the class action, assuming the suit is won or, more likely, settled out of court.

Because the law firm will use any public statement from the company's management in an attempt to show that management misled the investing public, executives become hypersensitive about saying anything about the future performance of the company. Worse, any article that has appeared in any newspaper or other publication, regardless of accuracy, will be used against management and the company if it helps the lawyers' case.

Another insidious problem is the current use − or abuse − of the Racketeer Influenced and Corrupt Organizations (RICO) law, a law intended to help prosecutors bring cases against mobsters. Now RICO is used extensively by people suing legitimate businesses. Bearing in mind all of these potential problems and risks, a company should choose its Board members, preferably from the "outside," wisely. And those who contemplate joining a Board should also choose wisely.

[Sahlman90] Sahlman, William A., "Why No Sane Person Should Serve on the Board of a Publicly Held Corporation," *Harvard Business Review*, No. 3, May-June 1990.

COMMUNICATING WITH WALL STREET

"Buy-side" and "sell-side" analysts have been the securities market's traditional scorekeepers, and they therefore create much of the quarterly pressure. They try to determine what corporate results are going to be, which isn't easy, based on the information available to them. With both types of analysts, timely and straightforward communication is key.

Buy-side analysts work for institutions or corporations that manage money. Like sell-side analysts, they attend company briefings, meet with management and ask questions, but they generally keep their views to themselves. Their primary interest is to determine whether they should recommend the purchase of a new issue or add to or sell their current holdings in a company's stock. One money manager, Sheldon Claar, was unique in that he was always very concerned that I come out of the process in good financial shape. He had seen too many entrepreneurs come out with nothing.

Sell-side analysts work for brokerage firms, and their goal is to generate commissions for their respective companies via the purchase or sale of securities as a result of their recommendations. Each aspires to be the top analyst in his or her field, based on an annual survey of the readers of *Institutional Investor* magazine. In contrast to buy-side analysts, sell-side analysts like visibility. As part of this publicity effort, they prepare written reports for distribution to brokers, institutions, prospective clients, media and other interested parties. Sell-siders also hold seminars featuring the companies they follow in order to "showcase" them to prospective buyers.

The worst thing that can happen to a sell-side analyst is to be surprised. Consequently, sell-side analysts aggressively pursue the executives of every company that they follow to make sure that their estimates of projected quarterly and yearly revenue and profits turn out to be accurate.

The issue of insider information is very much a gray area in this atmosphere. For example, many Chief Financial Officers feel obligated to "talk" analysts off some overly optimistic or pessimistic estimate. Otherwise, the analysts will feel that they have been misled and might develop a negative view of your company. Any such pejoratives will hurt the stock price of a company and might even be used by competitors in their sales efforts.

Some sell-side analysts get too close to companies and their management. They may become so bullish or negative on a company that their reputations become intertwined with the company's performance. Sell-side analysts may even help contribute to a self-fulfilling prophecy via their reports when these reports are used in competitive situations by the companies that they are promoting versus companies that they are not.

Nevertheless, the best way to communicate with Wall Street is to be honest and tell everyone the same thing at the same time. The way to do this is to conduct a meeting for all analysts every quarter, as close as possible to when your financial results are available.

> *Wall Street, like everybody,*
> *likes to be treated honestly.*

It's also good to realize that the analysts following your company are usually very bright and have many contacts within your customer base or even within your company. Management would be wise to listen to their questions and opinions carefully. The Company was often singled out in the software industry as the model to follow in communicating with Wall Street. The reason is, I believe, that we followed the above plan religiously, in good times and bad.

CHANGING OF THE GUARD

Running a publicly held firm with a quarterly focus, even as successful as the Company had become, was not a very enjoyable long-term career path, and I was planning to move on.

So, in 1981, as a first step leading to a "changing of the guard," I formed a management committee comprised of four individuals with combined management, technical, financial and marketing skills. The group worked very well. I was delighted with it because we could make decisions very fast. However, I was surprised to learn that a lot of other people in the Company were not as delighted.

In the past, I would talk to many people in the hallways to get their opinions about something the Company should be doing or was thinking about doing. I would take their advice seriously and operate accordingly. Consequently, many employees felt they had a real say in what the Company did. Now, with the establishment of the committee, they felt left out – the theory of the unanticipated result again.

An entrepreneur should plan

for his succession,

or someone else will do it for him.

Nonetheless, in March 1983, Bob Goldman was elected President. I continued as Chairman of the Company, but to give Bob space, I moved to offices in downtown Boston and became involved in many community and charitable affairs.

First, however, the Company's name was changed from Cullinane to Cullinet Software, Inc., anticipating the great emphasis on the networking of computers that was obviously going to take place in the future. It was done so that I could get my name back, as well. Who knew what might happen in the future?

If I had it to do all over again, I would have left the Company completely. I think one foot in and one foot out doesn't do anybody any good. Yet, I wanted to make sure everything was solid before I cut the cord.

GOLDEN PARACHUTES

With the advent of unfriendly corporate takeovers in the 1980s, some Wall Street law firms and investment bankers created some imaginative defenses, among them poison pills, shark repellents and golden parachutes. These techniques, which were rarely successful in preventing a takeover, were designed to make the takeover as difficult and expensive as possible.

A case can be made that management of a corporation that had been in trouble but was on the road to recovery as a result of management's hard work was particularly vulnerable to an unfriendly takeover. Those in top management positions would lose their jobs while the acquiring company would benefit from their work. A golden parachute was designed to protect management in such a situation and have the added protection of making the takeover that much more expensive.

> *Golden parachutes*
>
> *create the potential*
>
> *for conflict of interest.*

However, when a company is in trouble, a small group of executives positioned to receive millions in golden parachutes if the company is sold presents serious potential for conflict of interest. It may be much more attractive for some managers to reason, "Why bother with the misery of trying to turn the company around? Why not just sell it, collect my million dollars and go on to a better, new job with a successful company and leave all the headaches behind?"

This would be a formidable rationale for many managers, particularly if they had little loyalty to a company. Therefore, the future of a company should not be arbitrarily determined by a small group of executives who will receive huge, short-term benefits from its sale, regardless of their contribution.

WALL STREET REVISITED

In the late 1970s and early '80s, my impression of Wall Street was that they were all crazy; the reason that they didn't know it was that they spoke only to each other. Retaining one's sanity under the day-to-day pressures of whether the market is up or down at that moment is no long-term career path for anybody, in my opinion. Corporate executives, including myself, complain of quarterly reporting. What must it be like to live and work under real-time reporting? That is why humor, however sick it may be at times, is so appreciated on Wall Street. It's an escape valve.

Unfortunately, in the '80s, Wall Street took a sinister step backward to the '20s as the "get government off our backs" mentality permeated many of the regulatory agencies and those they were supposed to regulate. While the SEC did not have responsibility for regulating the savings and loan industry, things were happening that, ultimately, would have disastrous consequences for all of us. In the early 1980s, savings and loans institutions were given the opportunity to grow out of their problems by going into just about any business that they chose to, and their depositors couldn't lose any money. This was because their deposits were insured by us, the taxpayers. It was a sweetheart situation for all the "fast-buck artists." It would only be a matter of time before they took advantage of the situation and the savings and loans became "players" in the roaring '80s.

Wall Street needs strong regulation

to succeed.

Meanwhile, back on Wall Street — or, to be more accurate, in Los Angeles — out of sight or review of corporate headquarters or any governing body, was emerging a "Junk Bond Exchange." What was unusual about this exchange was that one person had total control of it. He created it, ran it like a personal fiefdom, and corporate headquarters was loathe to interfere with their star performer, who generated so much profit for everybody. Failure to do so would eventually cost them their company and the loss of ten thousand jobs. What their star performer had determined, as others had, was that some junk bonds weren't as risky as many thought. The real problem was that they were difficult to trade.

Looking for new opportunities, it occurred to him that junk bonds could be used to finance leveraged buyouts of American corporations. William Simon, former Secretary of the Treasury, had already demonstrated the potential of a leveraged buyout. Armed with this commitment to raise vast amounts via junk bonds, no American corporation was immune to takeover by anybody, regardless of qualifications or track history. As a result, they struck fear into the hearts of corporate America while making awesome amounts of money.

The net result was that a lot of American companies were put "in play," and a lot of the junk bonds ended up owned by savings and loan institutions. Ultimately, a few people ended up in jail, a few made enormous sums of money while hundreds of thousands lost their jobs as the corporate raiders cut costs to improve cash flow in order to meet the interest payments on the huge debt. Some took their companies public again in order to reduce debt and made even more money.

No wonder that the richest one per cent of Americans' share of the American pie has increased from eight per cent to four-teen percent in recent years. This, while many corporations have been dismantled, and we, the taxpayers, have been stuck with a 500 billion dollar bill to bail out the savings and loan institutions. A big part of this bill is due to the worthless junk bonds bought through the Junk Bond Exchange.

I don't think many people appreciate the carnage brought to the American financial system by, essentially, one person and his friends. The reason that so much securities legislation was written in the 1930s was to prevent the recurrence of the 1929 stock crash that was brought about, in part, by the manipulation of a few to the detriment of many. It's sad that we never learn from history. Anyone wishing to learn more about these topics might read *The Greatest-Ever Bank Robbery* by Martin Mayer [Mayer90] and *Den of Thieves* by James B. Stewart [Stewart91].

Ironic here is that the Wall Street firm that raised the original funds for the Cullinane Corporation was Burnham & Co., later to become Drexel, Burnham, Lambert of junk-bond fame. The investment banking firm that arranged the sale of the Company was the prestigious firm of Goldman, Sachs, both prominent in James Stewart's book.

[Mayer90]   Martin Mayer, *The Greatest-Ever Bank Robbery*, Charles Scribner's Sons, New York, 1990.

[Stewart91]   James B. Stewart, *The Den of Thieves*, Simon & Schuster, New York, 1991.

CORPORATE GOVERNANCE

There is currently much turmoil in the area of corporate governance that will impact corporate managements in the future. The recent landmark action of General Motors' Board of Directors and its counsel, Ira Millstein, of reducing its Chairman's power is a harbinger of things to come.

There are many changes coming in corporate governance.

Many such actions are the results of pressures on corporate poor performers from large investors such as pension funds. Their involvement will only hasten the process of Boards' becoming more involved in management decisions.

The prevailing view among experts of corporate governance is that too many Boards of Directors have been too friendly to management and that there are changes in the air. Among the possibilities are, for example:

- Corporate Boards will consist of fewer members.

- Each Board member will be highly experienced in one or more facets of the company's business and industry.

- Each member will have to be able to spend much more time on company problems and issues than is currently the case.

- Each member will receive much more compensation than he or she does now.

- Large investors such as pension funds will be much more proactive regarding management compensation, performance and related benefits, including bonuses, stock options and golden parachutes.

- The role of the Chairman of the Board/Chief Executive Officer will be clearly differentiated from that of the President of the Company/Chief Operating Officer. Today, the Chairman/CEO's role vs. the President/COO's role is confusing, even to a company's employees.

Additionally, my personal recommendation would be that quarterly reporting be changed to six-month reporting, similar to other countries' requirements. This would still protect the investors' need to know on a timely basis while allowing management to spend more time on competitive issues.

I also believe that the six-month report should include an audited survey of what customers and prospects think about the company and its products and/or services and a comparison of the results with those of the previous six months. Monitoring changes would be enormously valuable to an investor, regardless of sophistication, and would be a great incentive for management to correct problems in time for the next survey.

MANAGING THE WALL STREET EXPERIENCE

1. Investment bankers are not known for their loyalty; they are interested in big fees, regardless where they come from.

2. Underwriters are interested in their clients, particularly institutions doing well via your stock; therefore, they would like to price your stock low to reduce not only their (underwriter's) risk but improve the possibility that their clients will do well with your stock and, therefore, buy the next deal coming down the pike.

3. Wall Street thinks of you and your company as merchandise; they don't care about your clients or employees. As such, they are what I refer to as an "unnatural" constituency.

4. Tell everyone on Wall Street the same thing at the same time via quarterly financial analysts' meetings.

5. Treat Wall Street people honestly. Their careers are at stake, and a lot of their customers' money is on the line.

6. Don't expect Wall Street to be sympathetic to your problems. After all, chances are that you have made a lot of money via Wall Street, and it comes with a price.

7. Don't manage to the quarter; make this clear to Wall Street in the beginning. Expect your stock to take a hit as a result, but over time it will reach its appropriate value relative to its competitors.

8. Remember, Wall Street is really like one big gambling casino. Don't play games with your stock. Keep your eye on your customers and the bottom line, and let the stock take care of itself.

Chapter Five

The High-Tech
Success Syndrome

THE END OF THE HARDWARE ERA

By 1983, competitive pressures on our IDMS database management system and flagship product were building. The major reason was that we continued to consider relational and SQL technology inappropriate for high-performance production systems. Also, we had not yet introduced products that recognized the importance of personal computers. We had to respond, or else we were in danger of being hurt badly.

Our solution was to have a national teleconference on April 19, 1983, to announce major new products. As a prelude to this teleconference, we implemented an incredibly aggressive advertising campaign announcing "The End of the Hardware Era." The beginning of the software era would take place on April 19, with full, multiple-page ads in *The Wall Street Journal* and trade publications. In retrospect, it was a pretty accurate forecast of the developing importance of software. It created great interest and something of a furor because no one knew what we planned to announce.

The press conference and analysts' meeting were teleconferenced to 16 cities that represented about 3,000 prospects and customers and included a live interview with Steve Jobs announcing a joint venture featuring Apple and the Company. It was a great success. The message was that the Company was introducing a relational version of IDMS, an Information Center System and a personal computer integrated package called Goldengate. Our customers and prospects loved the announcements, and they held the market for two years. As a result, we continued to grow at an annual rate of 50%.

But despite its great success, there were two fundamental problems with this announcement. The first was that we had neglected to brief the trade press in advance of the announcement. Since there was great interest, they were under pressure from their editors to find out what it was. No one leaked the story, and they were completely left in the dark. The result was that they were furious at us. This was not done intentionally; we had just never thought about them as we had never worked closely with the trade press in the past.

A strategy,

to be effective in the long term,

has to be based on substance.

The second was that there was something basically wrong with this flashy announcement. We weren't demonstrating these products; we were playing catch up. We were "preannouncing" – something IBM had done for years – what was known as "vaporware" in the software industry.

WHAT WAS THE PROBLEM?

The Company should not have needed the April 19th announcement; we had never needed one in the past. What is ironic is that, in 1980, I had been asking our technical people why we couldn't have a two-database strategy, which would have included a relational database management system. I had thought, to cover our bases, the Company should invest in a relational database startup.

*Jon Nackerud, then a Company Vice President, was planning to leave to start such a company and asked if the Company would like to invest. We met with the founders but I didn't have a good feeling about their business acumen. They were all professors and researchers at a major university. Consequently, we didn't invest. This firm, called Ingres, ultimately became a major player in the relational market but with a spotty financial track record. It was eventually acquired by ASK Computer.

The potential of new relational technology to generate the necessary revenues to keep the Company growing at a rate of 50% was, admittedly, very questionable in 1980, particularly in the mainframe market.

It's important to understand

what business you are in.

In 1981, the Company introduced a powerful 4th-generation language, developed by *Dave Litwack, that would allow us to build the first 4th-generation applications by integrating database, applications and decision-support systems. I chose this route personally for growth reasons. While the Company had a lot of trouble implementing these applications, the three-level integration of database, applications and decision-support systems was a very successful strategy from a marketing point of view; it put competitors on the defensive. But an unanticipated result was that all our technology was becoming increasingly proprietary and not portable to other computers, at a time when the move to open systems architecture was just getting underway.

Jon Nackerud: Jon is covered in a separate chapter.

David Litwack: Prior to the development of the ADS/OnLine fourth-generation language, David was a key developer of the Company's IDMS-DC telecommunications monitor, along with Nick Rini and Don Heitzmann. David has recently built a Windows-based 4th-generation language for Powersoft, Inc.

DOWN QUARTER

Even though sales and profit figures continued to be spectacular during 1983, 1984 and 1985, one could sense that things weren't getting easier. However, one hoped business would continue to grow as it had for the past thirteen years.

During the first quarter of Fiscal Year 1986 (May-July), we were concerned enough about revenue prospects for the quarter to send out a news release to this effect. However, we thought we could make our traditional profit goals of 20% to 22% before taxes right up to the last day, but we didn't. Our 29-quarter streak of 50% growth in sales and profits had come to an end.

When the second quarter in the Company wasn't much better, I became quite concerned and took on a much more active role again. First, we eliminated the more complex forecasting system that had evolved and went back to our traditional, simple forecasting method. The new forecasts showed that the third and fourth quarters were going to be very tight. We immediately instituted a hiring freeze and began working on increasing sales via an Executive Management Day. This seminar required the Company's executive management to go on the road to major cities across the country in late December and January to present the Company's present and future strategy to customers and prospects.

We rented a private jet for the back-to-back meetings in Detroit, Chicago and Cleveland. The seminars were very successful and proved instrumental in the Company having a strong fourth quarter. We made a $15 million profit for the year on essentially flat year-to-year sales. I've always felt this was a remarkable accomplishment based on recognizing a problem and moving fast to cope with it. We caught expenses in time and increased revenues in the third and fourth quarters. It was indicative of how fast and effectively the Company could still move when it had to.

However, for the first time in many years, IBM put us on the defensive by introducing a new database system called DB2, a move also to protect their IMS customer base, which had begun to switch to our Company's database management system in increasing numbers. While DB2 lacked most of the sophisticated tools of the Company's database management system and wasn't well-suited for high volume, transaction-oriented processing, it didn't make enough difference to a prospect.

> *Going back to fundamentals*
>
> *always seems to work -- for a while.*

In reality, though, DB2 only compounded the problem for IDMS. Of major concern were the database saturation of the mainframe market and the slowdown of mainframe sales and the proprietary nature of IDMS in an era when customers wanted hardware and software independence. For all these reasons, our market niche was closing much faster than we ever thought possible.

Unfortunately, it wasn't an "aberration," as I thought at the time. We were in trouble, and some "magical" solution had to be found.

NEW MANAGEMENT

During this period of more intensive personal involvement in the Company's affairs, I had the sinking feeling that it had developed some fundamental problems. Perhaps we had grown somewhat complacent. We also had developed some major problems we had never had in the past, including a lawsuit with a software vendor that, unfortunately, was lost. Our efforts in the personal computer market with Goldengate got off to a great start but fizzled.

All the years of great success and growth had come with a price. We were having trouble implementing new products and developing a new strategy. As a result, we weren't positioning our products as well as we used to.

There is an old industry saying that God was able to rest on the seventh day because he didn't have an existing user base to accommodate. A user base really complicates moving to new technology. It's not that you don't know what to do; it's figuring out how to get there that can be really frustrating.

In addition, with the mainframe market slowdown, we were going to have to enter new, non-IBM markets and become much more aggressive in the international markets, particularly in the Far East. I knew that the Company needed a significant infusion of management experience in running large, international corporations.

Consequently, I cast about for someone who had considerable experience in IBM and non-IBM markets, as well as in the international arena, to replace me as CEO. I found what seemed to be the ideal candidate, and he came highly recommended. I convinced him to take the position of Vice Chairman and CEO of the Company, while I remained as Chairman.

Off-loading problems

always comes back to haunt you.

I had no intention of getting back on the quarterly treadmill although, in retrospect, it would have been much easier if I had.

We still had $50 million in the bank and only 1700 employees. I strongly urged our existing executive management team to stay and learn because they were young, but they chose to leave. In retrospect, I couldn't blame them; their reporting structure had been changed. However, it certainly didn't make my job any easier.

Incidentally, changing the management structure in a publicly held company is an extremely delicate process. Any leak can cause havoc with the stock, as well as impact all the people who are involved.

MOVING ON

It's quite amazing how fast a corporate culture can change.   It wasn't long before I could hardly recognize the Company anymore. For example, some months before one of the Company's new sales conferences, I had watched a television interview of a college basketball coach with a questionable ethical record. He was asked what he did while not coaching. When he stated that he spoke at corporate sales meetings, etc., I wondered, "What company would possibly hire this coach to speak at its meetings?" Well, I went to one of the Company's sales meetings, and — you guessed it — the coach was speaking.

It was time for me to move on. In June 1987, I announced my intention to retire from both the Company and the Board of Directors as of the Annual Meeting in the fall. Then, in September 1987, after the Annual Meeting was over, I just walked out of the room and had lunch with my wife and her mother.

> *A year should be made up*
>
> *of four seasons,*
>
> *not four quarters.*

It felt like a great burden had been lifted from my shoulders. For the first time in 20 years, I wasn't going to have to worry about the Company anymore. I was free to do anything I wanted. I could actually think of a year being made up of four seasons rather than four quarters.

Unfortunately, I didn't get through one season before I was involved in the Company again in a way that I never intended. The symptoms of the high-tech success syndrome were indicating far more serious problems than we realized.

THE HIGH-TECH SUCCESS SYNDROME

I once was invited by an acquaintance to look at his property on Cape Cod that was for sale. As he showed me around the house, we passed a model of a huge ship enclosed in glass. It looked like the Queen Mary. When I asked him whose ship it was, he answered that it had been, at one time, the family yacht. It seems his family, who were in the coal business, were cruising on the yacht one day when they received an urgent message that the coal had just run out. That was the end of the yacht, which was sold to the Philippine government and, ultimately, sunk by the Japanese in World War II.

The high-tech success syndrome is very much like owning a coal mine or any other mine. Things can be great but, once the ore runs out, the game is over, and it can happen, literally, overnight. By the 1980s, the Company had no reason to be concerned about the syndrome. In fact, we didn't even know what it was. We did know that sales and profits continued to grow at a remarkable rate. In addition, the Company had just completed building what, in my opinion, was the most advanced set of fourth-generation applications ever created.

Our strategy was to buy applications with the best functions on the market, such as a general ledger system from McCormack & Dodge and a manufacturing system from Rath & Strong. We then completely rewrote the applications using our database management system as the foundation. In addition, the $30,000,000 we had invested in the most advanced integrated banking system was just about to bear fruit. This meant that all our applications shared common data or "talked" to each other, a tremendous competitive advantage for us and our clients. Also, these applications were fully integrated with decision-support systems and other PC-based products such as advanced installation and training technology. Customer surveys conducted by research houses indicated a very strong buyer preference for these applications.

It was a huge and very expensive undertaking but all funded out of earnings. The result was that the combined selling prices of our product offerings, not counting the Banking System, increased from $300,000 in 1981 to $3,500,000 by 1985. The Banking System sold for $2,000,000, and we were becoming a product-rich company. We were becoming a single source of comprehensive software products for major corporations around the world. Our competitors were afraid of us, as many software companies are afraid of Microsoft today. We had become the most powerful and successful software company in the mainframe software business with a seemingly great future.

We should have been in the catbird seat, but we weren't. Our dilemma was that we had all this great technology that hasn't been duplicated to this day, and we couldn't sell it. We didn't realize it at the time, but we had fallen into the trap of the high-tech success syndrome.

It is possible to be smart enough

to know you have the best products

and dumb enough not to know

that it doesn't make any difference.

-- *Jon Nackerud*

Our market niche had closed as it had for so many companies. For example, Wang Laboratories is an excellent example of nimbly avoiding this syndrome for many years, only to eventually get caught up in it. However, Wang is now making aggressive moves to recapture its traditional office-automation market, featuring image processing as the differentiator. Mohawk Data Sciences and Inforex caught the key to the disk niche but had trouble moving beyond it. Novell is in the communications niche. Data General has changed its niche from proprietary computers to open systems technology with some success, but it hasn't been easy.

The point is that every high-tech company operates in a niche. The Company's history shows that it was a mobile, market-driven company. For example, when our Culprit report generator niche wasn't selling well, we moved into the EDP Auditor niche. From there, we went into the database management system niche, then into the integrated software tools niche, then into integrated applications and the PC software niche. Then, the mainframe niche ended, and our opportunities quickly came to a halt. For fifteen years, however, the mainframe software niche had been great.

Changes in management, acquisitions, etc. couldn't get the Company around this fundamental and dramatic change in the dynamics of the marketplace as start-ups came on stream with new technology featuring open systems architecture, many of them better positioned to take advantage of these new market niches. When I returned to the Company and became as deeply involved as I had during the 1970s and early '80s, it just became obvious to me. Why would anyone buy a mainframe system when roughly equivalent technology was available for 1/10th or 1/100th the cost and much easier to use or replace, to boot? IBM and many other vendors are struggling with this unpleasant fact of competitive life in the computer industry these days.

My eventual conclusion was that we would be wise to merge the Company at the best price possible. This we were able to do, but it was a very close call. First, though, we were still in for some very bad times.

THE MISSING CHIEF CUSTOMER ADVOCATE

John Sculley, Chairman and CEO of Apple Computer, recently created a new position entitled Chief Technology Officer and assumed this position, also. I knew immediately why he had done it. John, I believe, has recognized how easy it is for the technical arm of a high-tech company to get out of synch with corporate strategic directions. In other words, a company can end up building what its technicians think the customers *ought* to buy instead of what their customers *want* to buy. Worse, a company can end up selling what it isn't building.

While John may call it the Chief Technology Officer and I call it the Chief Customer Advocate, the intent is the same, to prevent such a divergence from taking place. I first became aware of this syndrome early in the Company's existence and caught it in time to prevent the Company from going bankrupt.

Committing to develop file-matching facilities for Culprit and then for its EDP Auditor version saved the Company. Betting the Company on IDMS, committing to the Integrated Data Dictionary, undertaking a study of back-end database management systems for three government agencies and then building the first prototype of such a system, and the decisions to build a state-of-the-art teleprocessing monitor (rather than buy an existing system) and to go into applications were initiated by me in the role of Chief Customer Advocate.

Some of the above were results of listening to knowledgeable customers like Larry Towner of Naval Intelligence or industry consultants such as Bob Curtice of Arthur D. Little, Inc. – and, of course, key employees. In other cases, decisions were based on just an intuitive "feel" for what the Company should be doing. Some products, like the Integrated Data Dictionary, actually required finding an imaginative way around the objections of our overworked development staff. Fortunately, our staff, once convinced, was wonderful at building these systems. Of significance is that the above product examples were virtually all of the major technical initiatives of the Company between 1971 and 1981, and all worked out extraordinarily well. However, despite all our tools, applications were much more difficult to build than I had anticipated.

Implementing the prototype back-end database management system would also prove to be a very difficult technical feat. As a result, I took a lot of flack for having committed the Company to creating a system that had never been built before.

After this effort, our staff concurrently created a completely new version of IDMS, an Integrated Data Dictionary and a teleprocessing monitor, all designed to work together in an elegant fashion. The result was a marvelously efficient and sophisticated database system. This new version would be key to our great financial success in subsequent years. It wasn't until a long time later that one of our key technicians let it slip that they learned how to build this system from having built the back-end database machine. Up until that moment, I had been feeling guilty about that decision and all the agony I had put some staff members through. Nevertheless, my relationship with our technical staff was always good because I appreciated what they did and put the spotlight on them whenever possible, such as at User Weeks.

However, the point is that, without appreciating how important this contribution was, I had been functioning as the Company's Chief Customer Advocate since its founding. I certainly knew it was hard work. In fact, it was often like a technical "tractor pull." As a non-technician, I questioned whether I should be making so many key, product decisions. The technology was becoming so complex and varied that I felt it was like playing Russian Roulette.

Thus, by 1980, when Application Development System (ADS), a new system developed by Dave Litwack, was in its final testing phase, I was particularly sensitive to this issue. ADS was an on-line, fourth-generation language that would prove very successful but, unlike the above examples, I had absolutely nothing to do with the decision to build it.

The Chief Customer Advocate

has to be a CEO with a

strong commitment to the customer.

The fact that a system could be developed without my involvement in any way only confirmed my belief that someone with a technical background should be making these decisions. While the potential of this new product was critical to my decision to enter the applications business, it would end my role as the Company's Chief Customer Advocate.

It was time to acknowledge the need for a different kind of player, a technician-businessman. This, plus the fact that I was totally disenchanted with running a company on a quarterly basis, convinced me to make some fundamental changes in how the Company would be managed in the future.

Yet it seemed, from then on, the position of the Company's technical spokespeople to requests for a technology such as relational was that it was slow, couldn't handle high-volume production systems and wouldn't be practical until the advent of content-addressable storage. The SQL technology necessary for open systems architecture was barely mentioned. They were, I believe, accurately reflecting the needs of the customers with whom they interfaced because the number one reason why new systems fail is lack of performance.

In retrospect, the counterbalance necessary to reflect the total needs of customers, prospects and the corporation wasn't there anymore. There was no Chief Customer Advocate with CEO authority looking after the interests of the customers as the *customers* perceived them — again, the theory of the unintended result.

This phenomenon would continue after the acquisition of Computer Pictures Corporation, whose executive information system had sold many millions of dollars of the Company's software at the CEO level. My intent was that its staff would move this software to the personal computer and that the result would be products, as well as an experienced staff to capitalize on this new, fast-growing market.

Ideally, what would come out of this acquisition was to be an executive information system — or better still, PC-based development tools. However, in the absence of a Chief Customer Advocate, what emerged was not what I had anticipated but rather an integrated system similar to Lotus's Symphony product, called Goldengate. We caught the great movement to PCs at precisely the right moment with the wrong product.

The answer to why would come when I returned to the Company and began to really dig into what the Company was developing. It became painfully obvious to me that we had fallen into the old *we-know-what's-best-for-our-customers* trap again. It happened during a heated exchange between me and some of the Company's top technicians. The problem had to do with a new, all-purpose release of IDMS, which had been under development for years, yet didn't solve the competitive issues of the day.

One key technician said that, in the future, he would get all our customers in one room and prove to them that he was right! I responded by saying that, by the time it happened, there wouldn't be anybody in the room! The sad part was that this person was an outstanding technician, worked extremely hard and truly cared about customers. It wasn't his fault.

The problem was that no one with the authority and total responsibility for the best interests of the corporation was making product decisions. No CEO would let the sales department unilaterally make strategic decisions for the company. Why should the technical department do so? It is the responsibility of the CEO to understand that various departments can have different motivating factors and to organize the company to accommodate them.

I doubt that our technicians or anyone else in the Company would have had a problem with a Chief Customer Advocate if they had believed it was good for the Company; they were a very unselfish group. However, my experience strongly suggests that the CEO has to be the Chief Customer Advocate. Only a CEO has the authority to marshall all corporate resources in favor of the long-term interests of the company, which are unequivocally linked with the best interests of the client – as interpreted by the client, not by one's staff. Anyone running a high-tech firm would be well advised to heed this experience.

Just for the record, *I* was the CEO.

WAYS TO MANAGE INTO THE HIGH-TECH SUCCESS SYNDROME

1. Assume that the good times will last forever.

2. Fail to recognize that a high-tech success syndrome exists.

3. Fail to appreciate that the sales of high-tech products can cease, literally, overnight.

4. Fail to appreciate that a niche market will last only until the next competitive niche appears.

5. Fail to realize that many of your employees are so emotionally committed to your (their) products that they can't objectively evaluate new, competitive technology.

6. Fail to appreciate that it is extremely difficult to enter these new niche markets with your existing organization.

7. Fail to realize that it is easier for a start-up company to fill a new niche than your company can.

8. Fail to recognize that knocking the new technology is no solution.

9. Fail to recognize that, no matter how good your products are, it may not make any difference.

10. Fail to recognize that what the customer wants to buy is what you're in business to build.

Chapter Six

Managing in Bad Times

SECOND THOUGHTS

Being a bystander while the Company continued to struggle was difficult. With a personal as well as a financial investment in the Company, I couldn't stand on the sidelines for long while the Company continued to lose vast sums of money. It was disturbing to read the quarterly reports in the local papers. Many people still held me responsible, even though I wasn't running things. It was a very uncomfortable position to be in. Besides, I was a major stockholder.

One continuing problem the Company had during this period was that costs were outstripping revenue. As part of the diversification program, the Company had begun to acquire many new companies, products, services and people. The Company had increased staff from 1,800 people to 2,500. Worse, the companies purchased in the diversification program were losing money and, since the Company was losing money too, the result was a disastrous financial performance. One Los Angeles company that was acquired even had a company dog and included its picture in the corporate brochure. Unfortunately, the company was also a dog and had to be closed down.

When our numbers came out after the second quarter (October 1987) and the Company was again far off target, it became obvious to me that there was no longer any justification for optimism. It was then that I decided to rejoin the Company's Board of Directors.

This led to a high-drama meeting on March 4th, 1988, when the Board appointed me Vice Chairman, with a broad mandate to turn the Company around if possible — or otherwise sell it. Then I was asked to develop a restructuring plan by April 29, which was, in my opinion, unfair to all parties involved. It seemed an impossible assignment because I had to create a restructuring plan that obviously wasn't going to include some members of the existing executive management team, while those same members of management were still in place. Their subordinates didn't know to whom to respond while executive management made every effort to keep their jobs. It would have been much easier for all concerned if all the executive changes had been made on March 4th, rather than waiting.

However, being a publicly held company requires a great deal of "covering your bases" in order to prevent subsequent lawsuits. At the March 4th meeting, I was tempted a number of times to say, "to Hell with it," but I knew that bankruptcy was a distinct possibility in the near future, and a lot of people can get badly hurt in a bankruptcy. It had to be avoided at all costs. In some ways, I felt like the pilot of that crippled DC-10 that crashed in Sioux City with a remarkably small loss of life. How could I get the Company "down" without a lot of people getting badly hurt?

Sometimes you have to do it yourself.

The next 18 months were the worst of my 30 years in business. I knew it was going to be very tough, but it turned out to be even tougher than I had imagined. In fact, it was such a depressing experience my Administrative Assistant said that I looked "gray." I certainly felt it. I had to force myself to go to work every day to a company that, sadly, I didn't recognize anymore, to convince a management team, mostly strangers, to do the difficult things that had to be done to keep this once great Company afloat. At such times, you'd like to have the luxury of blaming someone other than yourself for the predicament you are in. In my case, I could have left the Company in 1983, or I could have continued to run it the way I always had. Since I did neither, I was stuck with the results and had no one to blame but myself.

GETTING UP TO SPEED

It had been five years since I had been intensely involved in the Company. That meant I was going to have to relearn the organization, the business and, most importantly, the management, most of whom I didn't know. Unfortunately, I didn't have the time because it was obvious the Company had to be significantly restructured and that it had to be done fast. While revenues looked promising for the fourth quarter ending April 30, 1988, expenses were out of sight and getting higher. Cash was getting low, and there was no plan to cope with what I suspected would be a severe drop in revenues in the first quarter.

There seemed to be a sense of unreality in the Company that somehow, someone would lend us the money to continue or that sales of our new products would skyrocket and save the day. What the Company desperately needed was a very healthy dash of reality regarding potential revenue and a restructuring plan based on these conservative revenue goals. A restructuring plan is a euphemism for employee cutbacks, reduction in expenses, sale of products and/or divisions necessary to bring expenses in line with revenues.

In a turnaround situation,

it is imperative that you know

your management team well.

The first thing I did was to form a Management Committee of nine people. Four of them, Jon Nackerud, *Julie Donahue, *Doug Robinson and *Ann McArdle, were long-time Cullinet employees who knew the current version of the Company better than I did. I called it the "9s Committee."

At 4:00 p.m. on March 11, 1988, we met for the first time. I charged them with restructuring the Company while meeting a most conservative revenue goal. Besides, if they created the plan, they would be more prepared to implement it. This was a unique opportunity for them to do all the things they, and others, said we should be doing for a long time. They prepared the restructuring plan in time for a special Board of Directors meeting held on Sunday, March 20, 1988. I presented this preliminary version in summary form. A committee of the Board was established to review the plan and to further develop it, including deciding on a management organization to implement the plan, as well as a related staff reduction.

The members of the "9s Committee" submitted the final version of the plan at the April 29, 1988, Board of Directors meeting and the last working day of the fiscal year. The plan and its presentation so impressed the Board of Directors that they voted unanimously for it.

The next thing I did was sell the Company's only real estate investment, the "Lost Brook" development building in Norwood, Massachusetts, for $12,900,000. That was accomplished in three hours through a fortuitous set of events, and I believe we caught the Boston real estate market at its high. Most importantly, we then had some working capital to keep going for a year.

Julie Donahue: Julie had a great sense of what the customer wanted, but she had the incredibly difficult task of coping with the Company's many applications. She had inherited an extremely difficult situation and made the best of it. However, the pressure was so great that she was literally tilting to one side without realizing it. Julie is now Senior Vice President of Customer Services for D&B Software Services, Inc.

Doug Robinson: Doug was very young but the only financial guy we had in the Company. Yet, more than anyone, he rose to the occasion in a most difficult situation. Doug was eventually asked to join Computer Associates International, Inc., as a key member of their management team.

Ann McArdle: Ann was number two in the Company's Human Resource Department. She had inordinate good sense and used to caution how important it was to cut deeply enough. She currently has her own consulting business.

THE CUTBACK

The Company's restructuring plan was to be implemented on May 2, 1988. Part of the plan required a staff reduction of 400 good people who loved working at the Company. Cutting back staff is a painful process, no matter how you do it. People are hurt emotionally and financially if they don't have a job waiting for them. If done badly, though, cutbacks can generate a lot of negative publicity for a company. Fortunately, things were done so well that, even on the day of the layoff, some of the affected employees were quoted by the local press and electronic media as saying that the Company was "fair" in every way in how they went about the cutbacks, and that they were looking forward to attending the upcoming seminars on how to obtain new jobs and the associated job fair.

Being laid off is a terrible experience.

To help us plan, we hired a consulting firm that advised us on every detail. All management employees attended training sessions on how to cope with employees who were being laid off. They were extremely apprehensive about the chore but were encouraged by the training. Terminations were handled at 9:00 a.m. on Monday morning, May 2, 1988. After a brief initial meeting, all affected employees were asked to pack their belongings and leave the premises as soon as it had been completed.

The employees were strongly urged to attend special seminars that were beginning the next day. Our consultants, who were specialists in psychology, ran the seminars. These seminars gave ex-employees the opportunity to discuss their situation with peer groups, as well as provided guidance about job hunting and preparing resumes that best presented their accomplishments. The attendees, I was told, quickly got over their hurt and got on with the process of reselling themselves. Within a day or two, the reports started to come in on how much they liked the seminars, how valuable they were and how much they appreciated the effort the Company was making on their behalf.

Those employees remaining at the Company said that they were proud of the Company and that it was a "class" company for what it did and how it did it. It is interesting to note that the Company had often been referred to as a "class company" in the past, though I had not heard this phrase much in the last couple of years. Then we began to hear it again, often from both current and ex-employees. This was a development nobody anticipated but was an indication that maybe the Company was beginning to get back on track.

I know many companies up and down the Route 128 "high-technology belt" couldn't get over the amount of positive publicity we received from what is, in essence, a very negative story. Regardless of how well cutbacks are done, though, in any company they cause a tremendous amount of anguish. The key to lessening this anguish was that we really cared about our employees and tried to do right by them, and they knew it.

TELLING IT LIKE IT IS

After getting expenses in line, the next thing we had to do was solve the problem of our marketing strategy. That involved addressing the tough issues that had our customers concerned.

In June 1988, I said that we must communicate the Company's strategy to as many customers and prospects as soon as possible because, for the previous few years, they had been hearing negative messages and unanswered questions from our competitors and the press. I suggested an Executive Management Day, which had worked well in the past, as the vehicle to communicate our message. As we had done before, the Company's executive management would visit major cities and discuss all issues related to the Company's financial status and future technical directions.

Some people thought we should wait until October so the attendance would be better. I said that I didn't care whether only 50 people showed up in New York in July; they would be 50 people who would hear our message that much sooner. Well, 175 people showed up in New York.

There was a lot of interest in what we had to say because most of these people had heard nothing directly from the Company in a long time. In fact, I put the toughest questions we had been hearing from all directions on the first slide of the presentation so the attendees would know we were serious. More importantly, it would force our management, technical and marketing people to come up with good answers. The first slide read as follows:

- What is the Company's financial status?

- What is the current status of its products and services?

- What is the future of IDMS/R?

- What is the Company's strategy regarding DB2?

- What about the Company's applications?

- What is the Company's technology direction?

- Why is Enterprise:Generator so important?

An important reason for committing to these eight cities, beginning in July, was that we were going to have to answer these tough questions in front of thousands of customers and prospects at our annual Users' Group meeting in September. Consequently, we were going to be forced to come to grips with issues such as Release 11 of IDMS/R, something we seemed incapable of delivering in recent years.

In tough times,

ask the toughest questions yourself.

IDMS Release 11 was the all-purpose solution to the relational and SQL issues. It was such a major technical undertaking that it was never clear what it was at any given time, nor was it ever finished. IDMS/R was, and is, the best DBMS with which to run a company, but customers and prospects wanted to know where we were going with it for the future, and they wanted relational and SQL capabilities. We had great difficulty in communicating an effective message, and it had hurt us badly.

Customers and prospects went home from the Executive Management Days saying, "Things are much better at the Company than we thought." They liked what they heard and the answers we gave them during the Question and Answer period. The eight-city tour was so successful that we added another eight cities in North America and five cities in five days in five countries in Europe, which were equally successful.

NEW STRATEGY

The Company's problem, simply stated, was that our flagship product, IDMS/R was a "lock-in" technology in the eyes of customers and prospects. No client or prospect wants to be locked in today, not to the Company and IDMS/R, not to IBM and DB2 or any other vendor. The customers and prospects wanted portable systems that allowed them to move to new, cheaper computers of their choosing.

In October, we had our Annual Company User Week in St. Louis with 4,000 attendees, followed by European User Week for about 750 people in Montreux, Switzerland. The plan for these meetings was to not only introduce the Company's new strategy but, most importantly, to demonstrate much of it.

The Company, with *John Landry's help, came up with a new strategy called *Enterprise Computing*. The Enterprise Computing concept had four categories — Database, Tools, Applications and Network Computing — built around the client/server model. Simply stated, client/server enables a user to use one computer (client) and access data on another computer (server). By establishing the Enterprise Computing concept, it was now easy to explain our new technology to customers and to convince them that IDMS/R had a future.

In my opinion, the Company's new Network Computing architecture, including Enterprise:BUILD and GENERATE, provided true portability and database/hardware independence better than any competitor. We had leap-frogged the competition. The architecture allowed a user to build high-level specifications, called PSRs, on one platform and communicate these specifications to any other platform. These specifications could then generate applications using any standard language and accessing any ANSI/SQL database management system. We were providing a truly open architecture. In the opinion of major clients, this was breakthrough technology. It allowed the Company and its customers to build their applications in a truly portable form in a client/server environment. This meant that a customer could now take advantage of, and economically justify the use of, different vendors' hardware or database management systems.

> *Companies often miss*
>
> *great strategy opportunities.*

Our customers and prospects were most impressed because we were able to demonstrate so much of this technology at our User Weeks. This was not vaporware. The Company was finally back on the offensive again. We had established a new playing field; as a result, we were able to put our competitors on the defensive, something we used to be very good at but hadn't done for years. One could feel the change that September, particularly after we came back from User Week.

During a breakfast meeting in St. Louis, one long-time client said to me, "I expect *you* to be enthusiastic, but when I went to the demonstrations of Enterprise Computing, we couldn't keep your technical people in their chairs, they were so excited. We were really impressed."

This enthusiasm started to permeate the Company. The grapevine is always very good at any company. You can't fool the employees. They knew they were onto something good, and it was beginning to show. With Enterprise:Generator and with proper positioning, we had "unlocked" IDMS/R and given our customers the option to select the best database management system, language and computer suited for the application. We had finally solved the problem by identifying it as "lock-in" and providing a tool that gave customers true freedom of choice. What is frustrating is that we could have easily implemented a two-database strategy with IDMS and a relational product including a COBOL generator tool back in 1980 and avoided a lot of the problems we eventually had. We also would have had a three-year lead on IBM and its IMS and DB2, a two-database system strategy.

One particularly difficult thing to cope with in situations such as these was the emotional one associated with the developers of the Company's software products. They had such a strong missionary zeal about "their" products that it was sometimes difficult for them to be objective about them.

John Landry: John joined the Company through acquisition of his company. John has an excellent sense of what is "hot" at that moment. He promoted the client/server model and was surprised that the Company was, in 1988, already 85% there. His positioning of Enterprise:Generator was important because it unlocked the proprietary characteristic of the Company's software. John became Senior Vice President of Technology at D&B Software and then left to join Lotus Development Corporation.

SETBACK

In difficult turnaround situations, you have to make sure that what you want done actually gets done the way you want. Despite the progress we made with our new product and marketing strategy, I soon discovered that key parts of the restructuring plan were not being implemented, and our numbers reflected this lack of compliance.

The first quarter of Fiscal Year '89 (May-July) was a severe disappointment. We did not generate our very conservative, "can't miss" sales goal as promised but fell $5 million short. We didn't have any room for such a miss. The second quarter showed some progress with a slight operating profit.

Unfortunately, the third quarter was far worse, with revenues considerably below our most conservative estimates. Unbelievable to me, expenses were $1,000,000 higher than budgeted.

One of the reasons was that 100 people had been hired in the second quarter. Why were we hiring people? How could we be expanding at such a critical time? It just was incredible that this could have happened. We were going to have to move fast again to cut costs by having another staff reduction.

Exasperated, I moved back to my old office at corporate headquarters and began to sit in on the day-to-day management meetings. I was in for a shock. I learned that a lot of the things I was led to believe were being undertaken as part of the May 2 restructuring just hadn't been done, such as establishing product ownership.

Product ownership is where one person has ultimate responsibility for a product and its success. The Company had 90 people in marketing, one for every salesperson in the field, with no one responsible for a product. In addition, such an organization located between development and sales only serves to confuse things and muddy the waters.

Never assume anything.

The follow-through on other important initiatives, such as actual cutbacks, just wasn't there, either. Someone had come up with the idea of "equivalents." An equivalent saving in some cost item meant that an agreed upon staff reduction didn't have to take place. This was just another method for avoiding tough decisions. Also, the classic mistake in reducing costs in a turnaround situation is to not cut back deeply enough.

I could go on, but the net result of the third quarter performance was that we had to give our investment banking firm the green light to sell the Company. Our year of borrowed time was almost up; we had one more quarter to go.

INFORMATION IS KING.

In view of our terrible performance, I took a pay cut. I decided to use the savings to get some analysis done to determine which of our products were actually making money and which weren't. Believe it or not, we did not have this very basic information.

At the time, some people in management believed that we were making money in applications and losing money in database, which I sincerely doubted. I hired a consultant, Tom Meurer, a former long-time Company employee. He proved conclusively that we were making $30,000,000 with IDMS and losing a similar fortune in both new product development and applications software.

All we had to do was determine how many people were assigned to each product and multiply by a cost-per-employee factor and then subtract this number from the product revenue to come up with the product profit or loss. This analysis was an eye-opener for many people in the Company. Tom also determined that, of the 72,000 man-days of consulting available in the field, the Company was giving away 42,000 of them. No wonder we were losing so much money.

> *In a turnaround situation,*
>
> *information is King.*

Complicating our potential fourth-quarter performance was poor communication with *The Wall Street Journal* regarding the necessary cut of an additional 300 people at the end of the third quarter. They felt they were misled by the Company about a second round of cuts and, as a result, *The Boston Globe* scooped them a couple of days later on the Company's planned cutback. They were very angry and absolutely crucified us in an article right after the cutback. Prospects for the fourth quarter looked grim, indeed.

To go from the most profitable software company in the history of the industry to the least in a very short period doesn't happen by accident. You have to work at it. All of this was so frustrating, personally, because the software products business, while very complex technically, is a very simple business.

FOURTH-QUARTER SUCCESS

We had only one quarter left to prove ourselves. After years away from running the Company on a day-to-day basis, I was back whether I liked it or not. More important, I now knew the business sufficiently well to start to make some tough decisions. First, I decided to implement the cut of 300 people at the end of the third quarter rather than wait until the end of the fourth quarter, even if it might impact the fourth quarter negatively. As part of the cut, I reduced dramatically the size of the 90-person marketing organization and established product ownership, part of the restructuring plan that had not been implemented.

A few days later, by chance, I dropped in on a meeting between the people who headed our Enterprise:Generator product development and some of our district sales managers, a meeting that would not have taken place under the previous organization. Our technical people were presenting a key new product, Enterprise:Generator for the mainframe and IDMS/R, to the district sales managers. This new product, critical to the Company's future, was going to be sent out at the end of our fiscal year, April 30th, undocumented and untested, and it required a new release of IDMS/R.

What was worse, the Company was forecasting that the product Enterprise:Generator would generate $5,000,000 in first-quarter revenues. I was appalled and just about to say how dumb that was when a district sales manager said, "This is really dumb!" Most agreed, including the product development people. After a few minutes, another district sales manager, Ed Rhodes, said, "Why don't we package Enterprise:Generator PC with it?" This immediately struck me as a good idea because a customer could try this new, breakthrough technology on the personal computer while waiting for the final release of the mainframe version, but still buy the mainframe version now. Most importantly, the PC version was a final, fully tested and beautifully documented version.

Subsequently, I created a trial plan, letter of intent and marketing package whereby a customer could acquire the products in the fourth or the first quarter under favorable terms. *Jeff Papows packaged this agreement and mailed them to all IDMS/R users. I was looking forward to excellent results.

By coincidence, a sales conference with a few select customers had been organized in Orlando. Approximately eighteen companies were represented at the conference. I decided to attend even though I was discouraged in so doing. However, I went anyway because this was a golden opportunity to test the effectiveness of the new marketing plan first-hand. I sat in the room all morning, waiting to hear the pitch for the plan. To my amazement, there wasn't any. Just as the meeting was about to close, I grabbed the mike and gave the best imitation of an Elmer Gantry sales pitch of my life. However, when I was finished and asked who was going to buy Enterprise:Generator, only four people raised their hands.

> *Good products, good strategy*
>
> *and aggressive promotion*
>
> *usually equal success.*

I was disappointed. This wasn't what I had hoped for or expected. However, as the meeting broke up, an unforeseen thing happened. A number of people came up to me in the hallway and apologized for not having raised their hands. They intended to buy the system but had to wait until they got back home to get formal approval. I was elated. Twelve of the eighteen eventually bought the system. This was a great percentage.

We sold 42 copies in the fourth quarter, a very small number, considering the above experience. However, as a result, we made a $2,000,000 profit in that quarter, the first profit in 13 quarters. The amount of profit exactly equaled the amount of revenue generated by the introduction of Enterprise:Generator in the fourth quarter.

Introducing a terrific new product in an imaginative way, while cutting costs at the end of the third quarter rather than waiting until the end of the fourth quarter, was also key to our success. Reducing costs and increasing revenue – how else do you make money? It seemed simple to me and something the Company had always practiced in "glory" years. However, our success was too little, too late, and the Company had to be sold. Nevertheless, making money would prove to be a big help when selling the Company.

Jeff Papows: Jeff is an incredibly hard worker and former "top gun" fighter pilot who headed up our marketing efforts. We put together an excellent marketing package and got it out fast. Jeff is now President and Chief Operations Officer of Cognos, Inc. of Burlington, Massachusetts.

A CORPORATE AUCTION

When a publicly held company is up for sale, it is often necessary to conduct an auction. Otherwise, management and the Board of Directors could be subject to a class-action lawsuit for having sold the company too cheaply. The role of the investment banker is not only to solicit buyers but to establish a value for the company that will withstand subsequent scrutiny.

The Company selected the New York investment banker Goldman Sachs, primarily for their overseas capabilities and outstanding reputation. In essence, we prepared a "book" about the Company, including all promotional material and related corporate descriptions. Goldman Sachs did the analytical work, comparing the Company's financial position with other organizations in the industry, for the purpose of valuing the Company. They also prepared A, B and C lists of prospective buyers. The A list contained the most obvious candidates. We then sent a copy of the book to all candidates, and Goldman Sachs contacted each directly.

The responses weren't too encouraging. Most of those that did respond were interested in acquiring parts of the Company's systems, such as applications. Since our products were tightly integrated, it was very difficult to do. Eventually, the obvious candidate (Computer Associates International, Inc.) expressed interest. They were the only company that was willing to acquire all the products. Having all the products supported by a single company only made sense and would be important to the Company's customer base.

> *Once the investment bankers are*
>
> *called in, your company is in play.*

Computer Associates acquired the Company for close to $400,000,000, and Goldman Sachs received an enormous fee. It's the opinion that is expensive because there was no deal until the head of Computer Associates, Charles Wang, and I got together. In fact, I have been told that Charles came to the meeting intending not to buy the Company. I don't know if this is true. While Charles Wang is a tough negotiator, I am pleased to say that he followed through in all his commitments to me. Sometimes it's important to know when to sell. In our case, we had no choice.

Most investors did well, and so did vendors. All bank loans were paid, all products stayed under one roof, and many of our employees retained their jobs. Those who didn't received the best severance package in the industry. Management received $12,000,000 in golden parachutes. Jon Nackerud, I learned later, refused to take one.

The Company was no more, but selling compared very favorably to bankruptcy, which had seemed inevitable in my opinion when I returned to the Company. The pain and losses that can be inflicted upon many corporate constituencies in a bankruptcy proceeding are formidable and to be avoided at all costs. Another option might have been to reduce the Company in size such that it could survive on annual renewal revenues plus a small amount of sales.

However, the dilemma was that the value of the Company might have dropped to $100,000,000 *if* it survived. Besides, the Company had no money to pay for termination costs. The corporation's Board of Directors had to consider the $400,000,000 opportunity as part of its responsibility to investors. Otherwise, they may have been subjected to class-action lawsuits from stockholders.

I had done a job that needed to be done, but it certainly wasn't any fun. The only satisfaction I got from it was knowing that I had not abandoned the sinking Company and that I had been able to steer it away from the horrors of bankruptcy.

THE JAPANESE CONNECTION

Right in the middle of the auction being conducted by Goldman Sachs, I received a fax from a top executive at Fujitsu. They wanted to meet with me but were very specific that they didn't want Goldman Sachs in attendance, which seemed like an odd request. I discussed this with Goldman Sachs and agreed to meet with Fujitsu representatives at a New York hotel.

In anticipation of the meeting, knowing of the Japanese fascination with the game of golf, I bought a number of gifts at The Country Club in Brookline, Massachusetts, where the U.S. Open Golf Championship had been held the previous year. It had some beautiful bronze etchings of the clubhouse and other memorabilia of the tournament. I planned to present a gift to each Fujitsu representative. The group was made up of a number of individuals who spoke English perfectly, with the exception of the senior executive, which is usually the case.

When I presented the gifts to them, a few were on the defensive because they had neglected to bring anything, but one representative, to the embarrassment of the rest of the group, condescendingly said, "So many Americans bring us gifts. When we open them, we find that they were made in Japan." As he opened the box with the bronze etching and turned it over to see where it was made, I asked, with some trepidation, what it said. To my relief, he answered, "Philadelphia."

What Fujitsu wanted in exchange for an investment in the Company was for us to sell Fujitsu computers to our customer base. Whether this would have been practical is open to question. Fujitsu has since entered into a similar relationship with the Canadian subsidiary of a U.S. database software company.

The amount of time that it would have taken a Japanese firm to decide on an investment was far longer than the time then available to the Company in view of the fast-moving developments with Computer Associates International, Inc. However, this particular relationship with Fujitsu only serves to illustrate that Japanese computer makers were, and are, having difficulties in selling large-scale computers. Consequently, they are searching for strategic relationships to help them compete with IBM, Amdahl, Hitachi and others.

> *The economics of computers*
>
> *applies to the Japanese, as well.*

What Fujitsu and, for that matter, IBM and other hardware manufacturers are having a difficult time coping with is that customers are no longer willing to pay up to $25 million for a difficult-to-use computer when they can buy a much easier-to-use computer for a fraction of the cost from other competitors.

THE LAST STOCKHOLDERS' MEETING

On September 12, 1989, a special stockholders' meeting was called to approve the sale of the Company. I didn't think any employees would attend. However, to my surprise, the auditorium was packed with employees, and others listened outside as loudspeakers broadcast the events. The employees had always understood what was going on in good times and bad.

It was all over in three minutes.

As I left the stage to walk out of the auditorium, the employees gave me a "standing ovation," according to the next day's *Boston Globe*. They knew that, even though I hadn't had an easy time during the previous 18 months, I had worked to protect their interests in negotiations with Computer Associates.

> *Most employees are remarkably loyal*
>
> *to a good company.*

The Company had always had a reputation for having the best people; that's why so many companies wanted to hire them. Yet, many of these employees were in tears as they realized that the end of a great company had just taken place. I was deeply touched by their show of appreciation because it was so unexpected. It made it all worthwhile.

POST MORTEM

It is easy to make excuses or find reasons why the Company eventually got into so much trouble after such a fantastic early success. Consequently, it would be worthwhile to compare the different performances of the Company in the Seventies versus the Eighties.

One excuse might be that the Company went public in 1978. The truth is that the Company was far more successful in every way for three years after it went public than before.

Another excuse might be that IBM murdered us with DB2 and a most effective marketing program. Well, actually, IBM had tried to kill us in the Seventies, and we became stronger for the experience.

A third excuse might be that the saturation of the mainframe market, combined with the move to less expensive computers and open architecture, rendered the Company's proprietary technology obsolete. My response is that a company should never get caught so out of synch with its customers' and its prospects' requirements.

A final excuse might be that the Company didn't spend enough money on research and development in the Eighties. In fact, the Company led the industry in R&D in the Eighties, yet did not create any significant new products. Worse, former employees like Nick Rini, were developing those products our customers had wanted to purchase for some time, such as performance monitors.

Ironically, in the Seventies, the Company, with a very small staff, turned out winner after winner. As a result, by 1981, the Company had become a powerhouse in the software industry. Robert Barker, a well-known investor, asked me at the Company's annual meeting what I felt was the Company's greatest strength. My answer was that the Company had no weaknesses. There are always problems and weaknesses in any company; it just happened, for that brief moment in time, we had them all under control, and the Company was humming like a beautiful machine. It was also very satisfying to know that the Company was viewed as the "class" company in the industry. The Company's customer base was so loyal that one competitor referred to it as a cult.

The momentum allowed the Company to continue to produce great financial success into the mid-Eighties. However, by 1981, I had "had" it. I had done my duty. All investors had made a bundle, and the Company was running like a top. Three years of dancing to Wall Street's quarterly tune were enough. I decided to form a management team, giving them the responsibility for delivering on the "numbers," with the intent of eventually turning the Company over to them and leaving.

In their first quarter, the management team almost didn't produce the expected results because some of their friends didn't deliver what they had promised, which came as a shock to the team. However, they learned their lesson well and produced outstanding financial results over the next four years. There was no question that they understood that their number one priority was to produce results. Nevertheless, these and other changes in management responsibility would impact the Company profoundly.

While, on the surface, you could barely notice a change, the balance of the Corporation had moved away from the customer. We still cared about our customers and prospects but, in the Eighties, seemed to be spending more time convincing them that we were right and they were wrong regarding what technology was in their best interests. What was ironic was that this same tendency had almost driven the Company out of business in its early days. Now, because there was no Chief Customer Advocate, no one in-house was insisting that the customers' needs be met or that another way be found to accommodate them, as we had so successfully done in the past.

As CEO, I should have anticipated the potential shift in the Company's focus and planned for it, but I didn't. After all, being "user-driven" was embedded in the Company's culture. However, seeds of the Company's later problems can, in my opinion, be traced to this organizational change.

What you don't do in 1992 could kill you by 1997 or sooner.

> *The fault, dear Brutus, is not*
>
> *in our stars, but in ourselves.*
>
> *-- Shakespeare*

My conclusion, from this corporate experience and from having played instrumental roles in founding a number of other very successful organizations, is that, while it is very difficult to nurture such ventures to health, it is very easy to destroy the delicate balance that created the success in the first place. The surest way to trouble for any organization is to forget that it is in business to satisfy its customers' needs. If you happen to be a CEO lucky enough to have built a successful organization, be very careful of how you change it. Regardless of your good intentions, there is always the specter of the "theory of the unintended result."

The easiest way to develop the will to champion your customers' interests is to think of your new car or nice house as a gift from them and, if you treat them right, they will make the mortgage payments, too. Given a chance, they will even pay for your children's education and your retirement.

Yes, customers are sometimes difficult, unreasonable or even exasperating, but as the old merchants of my childhood era were fond of saying, "The customer is always right." Odd, but I haven't heard this expression for about thirty years. American businesses are trying hard to relearn it.

The Company had to relearn it the hard way. My first challenge, on returning to the Company, was to get it refocused on the customer. Within 12 months, the Company demonstrated that it could make money again. Refocusing on the customer had been the first major step toward this elusive goal.

SO, WHAT'S THE MESSAGE?

There are 101 tips in this book but only one message. It is that, in any venture, *success comes from focusing on the customer*. When a company forgets this message or has never recognized it in the first place, it eventually fails or runs into hard times. It's that simple.

What makes the Company's story so valuable to any CEO is that it illustrates this point so clearly. For example, in its early days, the Company came perilously close to failing merely by not being responsive to customers' needs. It corrected itself just in time and focused on the customer as a way of corporate life. As a result, the Company experienced fantastic success for thirteen years in a row – until it repeated the mistake of its early days and came perilously close to going bankrupt again. Only by dramatically reducing costs and refocusing on the customer was it able to return to profitability and significantly increase the value of the Company prior to sale.

As a Fellow of the Center for Business and Government at the John F. Kennedy School of Government at Harvard, I wrote a paper entitled, "Widows and Orphans," which was a precursor to this book. It was a personal "walk-through" of the American financial system from the perspective of an entrepreneur.

After laboring on the paper for some time, I submitted it, to Professor John Dunlop, then acting Director of the Center and a respected professor in his own right. After reading it, he said, "It's like a *Canterbury Tale.*" I asked my son, who had recently been graduated from Harvard as an English major, what he thought Professor Dunlop might have meant. After a pause, my son said, "difficult to understand, but there's a message there."

What complicates the simple message of the importance of the customer are the two other, conflicting messages from the American financial system. One is derived from the legislation that created the Securities & Exchange Commission. It said that the investor, particularly the unsophisticated investor, was the most important constituency of the American financial system and had to be protected. The other message, so prevalent in recent years, is that management's sole responsibility is to maximize investors' return. I recently watched Sir James Goldsmith give a near duplicate of Michael Douglas's "greed-is-good" speech from the movie, *Wall Street*, to a television panel. He even berated a CEO on the panel by sarcastically asking if his company were in the business of doing good or making money for stockholders.

> *For you to succeed,*
>
> *your customer has to be King.*

"Doing good" for customers — at a profit, of course — is exactly what a company should be doing. It is the best way to maximize investor return. I know. A billion dollars was generated for investors by doing just that. Unfortunately, this simple but powerful message is often overwhelmed by the other two messages.

The American financial system could do wonders for America's competitive position in the world by clarifying the message that, when you buy a product from an American firm, you are King. There are easy ways to do this, and I believe they would work, but the Securities & Exchange Commission first has to update its legislation to reflect the importance of the customer.

MANAGING IN BAD TIMES

Always start with the worst-case

view of the future.

1. **Never attempt a turnaround without a team of people you know.**

   A turnaround is an intense, highly emotional experience. It tests everyone's ability. Thus, it is imperative that you have a strong sense of the loyalty of the people who are working with you. It is important that you can trust what they say. Otherwise, it may be too late to take corrective action once you find out what is actually happening.

2. **Get reliable information.**

   Knowledge is king in good times and bad. Accurate information in a turnaround situation is critical. You may have to hire a consultant to help get it. Often what has to be done becomes obvious once you have the information; it's just a matter of having the courage to do it.

3. **Understand that the software business is a very simple business.**

   While the software business may be complex from a technical point of view, it is actually a very simple business.

   ```
   TOTAL $ REVENUE   ÷  NUMBER OF EMPLOYEES  =  $ REVENUE/EMPLOYEE
   TOTAL $ COSTS     ÷  NUMBER OF EMPLOYEES  =  $ COST/EMPLOYEE
   ```

   Revenue per employee is supposed to be more than cost per employee. It's that simple.

Being inducted into the Academy of Distinguished Entrepreneurs, Wellesley, Massachusetts, 1984. Babson College was one of the first institutions to focus on the importance of entrepreneurship.

Some of the 4,500 attendees gathered for the Welcoming
Reception at the Company's User Week in Boston, October
1985. *(p. 48)*

Company officers and Board members watched the board as the first trade of a software company stock on the New York Stock Exchange was being flashed around the world, April 1982. *(p. 56)*
First Row, L to R: Cherry Goldman, Phyllis Swersky, Diddy Cullinane, Joe McNay, Rosie Grant, Bob Goldman.
Second Row, L to R: Myself, Bob Schmidt, Dick Block (who as a 24-year-old ensign taught Grace Hopper how to program), George White, Mary Eidson, John Donnelly.
Third Row, L to R: Pat Grant, Bill Eidson (partially hidden), unidentified guest, Lauri Fordham, Sol Manber (hidden), John Patterson, David Rubin.

My mother-in-law, Agnes Haverty, my mother, and Larry Broderick, a good friend, brought a personal touch to User Week social festivities. *(p. 167)*

My name up in lights in Las Vegas for the Company's User Week. By checkout time, they don't know who you are. *(p. 146)*

MANAGING IN BAD TIMES

4. Cash, Cash, Cash

Without cash, your company is bankrupt. It may be profitable on paper, but if you can't pay your bills, you are at the mercy of your creditors. Generate cash by every measure possible, including stretching accounts payable, collecting accounts receivable or factoring accounts receivable and implementing imaginative marketing programs.

5. When you cut back, make sure you cut enough.

The single biggest mistake most companies make is that they can never bring themselves to cut back deeply enough. What will surprise you is that your company will be more effective and efficient with the smaller organization than it was with the larger one.

6. Make a list of what is critical to survival and what's "nice to have."

There are some activities that are critical to survival and others that are not. Eliminate all things that are not directly related to generating revenue or delivery of the product. Everyone will try to convince you that their activity is critical, but most are just "nice to have."

7. Don't push products out the door.

There is a great temptation to release a product prematurely, but trying to generate much needed revenue by pushing products out the door before their time will only compound your problems and damage the company's long-term viability. Avoid this approach at all cost. It always comes back to haunt you.

MANAGING IN BAD TIMES

8. Develop a new product strategy. Communicate it.

After meeting with customers and prospects, develop a new strategy, based on the strengths of your product line, that addresses the perceived needs of customers and prospects. Prepare a presentation, and then go on the road and present it in a seminar format to as many key executives as possible.

Don't duck the tough questions. Make sure you have developed good answers that are supportable in fact. People will appreciate your efforts, and many will stay with you during difficult times. One of the reasons is that most of your customers have been through difficult times, too.

9. Focus on customers and prospects.

In difficult times, try not to pay attention to the negative stories published about your company. In fact, the best advice is: Don't read them. When the sun goes down, it is amazing how quickly people forget those stories or, for that matter, have never read them in the first place.

Concentrate on customers and prospects and on responding to their interests. They are the ones who are paying and will continue to pay the bills. Realizing this will make your job much easier.

10. Don't leave any skeletons in the closet.

Everyone appreciates being treated honestly and fairly, particularly in difficult times. They are more understanding of your problems than you may realize. Consequently, don't take advantage of them in the turnaround process. Regardless of the outcome, you will be glad that you didn't.

Chapter Seven

Management Mechanics

THE SYSTEM

If you step back far enough from any successful enterprise to look at it objectively, you will begin to recognize that a "system" exists. The system includes people and procedures that constitute a bureaucracy that has evolved with the growth of an organization, and it plays an important role in giving order to any company's activities. It creates and administers forms and procedures for tasks such as paying employees and vendors, paying taxes, hiring people and filing reports. However, the system can impede continued success because it takes on a life of its own and, like a parasite, can destroy the organization that gave it life.

The system is the enemy of change. It will begin to get in the way of management's ability to perform the functions that are vital to a company's survival, such as finding out if there is a problem, responding to customer needs and repositioning the company, all of which demand change.

As the company grows, the system begins to cut off communication between the customer and key decision-makers by creating multiple layers of management. When you have layers of management, such as a salesman reporting to a sales manager, reporting to a district manager, reporting to a regional manager, reporting to an executive vice president of sales, you can be sure that, by the time the information about a customer's needs works its way up the chain of command to the executive vice president or president, the information will have lost its sense of urgency, impact or accuracy. If there are problems, usually someone is at fault. Managers do not like to send problems up the chain but, if it has to be done, they make sure the problem appears less important than it is or that they are doing more than they really are.

Success will require learning how

to get around the system.

Many different ways have evolved to cope with the system, without managers, perhaps, realizing that this is what they were actually doing. A classic example is "management by walking around," made famous by Thomas J. Peters and Robert H. Waterman in *In Search of Excellence.* [Peters&Waterman82] Management by walking around means that an executive gets out of his office and walks around, observes and asks questions of those he meets. It's amazing what the executive will find out. It will often be the opposite of what the executive hears in the executive's management meetings. Being "user-driven," which is also described in the book, is another method of coping with the system.

Being user-driven is very important. This means meeting with a client or prospect face-to-face and coming away with a true sense of the problem and the customer's real frustrations or why the prospect isn't buying. It also means clearly appreciating how important it is for you to respond to the problem right away or else it may cost you dearly in new business with this prospect or poor references to prospective clients in the future.

The initial success of any entrepreneurial venture is usually based on a few good people who are able to act quickly and responsively. However, the system starts to take over quit quickly around the time the company reaches a size of 25 people or more. There begins the subtle process of moving decision-makers in an organization away from the customers, without even realizing it.

No one is immune to the problems created by the system, certainly not the Chairman of the Board or the President. The system inevitably pushes them into a "status symbol" position, isolating them from the daily realities of the company. They must not interfere with the regular structure of the organization, the system wants to say. Many managers feel that a perfect bureaucracy will solve all problems efficiently, but it just doesn't work that way.

Some of the approaches of coping with the system mentioned so far are useful, but they do not necessarily get to the heart of the problem. However, recognizing that the system exists is a good beginning.

[Peters&Waterman82]   T. J. Peters & R. H. Waterman, *In Search of Excellence*, Harper and Row, New York, 1982.

PROSPECTS ARE DIFFERENT FROM CUSTOMERS.

When a company is new, it has few customers and many prospects. By definition, the company is paying attention to prospects. When a company grows and has many customers, the balance can shift. It's important to be aware of this.

> *Prospects' interests are not always*
>
> *the same as customers' interests.*

As a result of learning how to cope with IBM and developing a good strategy, the Company continued to prosper and grow at a rate of 50% in both sales and profits and became the most successful software company of its time. Part of the key to our success, in addition to having good products, was that we paid attention to both customers and to prospects. The interests of prospects are often different from customers.

With the tremendous effort these days of being "user-driven," the distinction between prospects and customers can be missed as a company gains and acquires many customers. In fact, the customers of a software package can have vastly different requirements regarding volume, number of users, size of database, equipment, etc., than the prospects.

Actually, your competitors will often generate areas of interest for prospects based on their product strengths. In other words, vendors often create a need for new facilities or concepts that may or may not have value for the prospect while putting your company on the defensive. It's also possible for a software company to spend most of its development budget implementing customer requirements and forget about the realities of the marketplace.

THE THEORY OF THE NINES & SIXES

The most important step in coping with the "system" is identifying the "nines" and "sixes" in your organization. Assume there are no "tens."

So, what is a "nine," and what is a "six?" A nine is one of the corporate movers, a person who everyone in the company agrees is first-rate, has good judgment and cares about the company. Nines may be found anywhere in the organization. They anticipate problems and do something about them before they become crises. Successful companies have more nines than unsuccessful companies.

Sixes are big trouble. They look and sound like nines and know how to use the "system" to advance their interests. When a nine recognizes that something is dumb, he or she will ask why the company is doing it. In comparison, sixes will go along with a questionable policy because they think, "This was what management wanted," or "We've always done it this way." Sixes are really interested in themselves, not in the company or the customer. They are very dangerous to the long-term well-being of any company.

It's important to realize that you can never make a nine out of a six, unless you know how to manipulate DNA. These are fundamental character types, and changing them is not possible. One common solution is to send a six to a special program at some prestigious business school on the premise that more management training will help, or move them around in the company to positions they supposedly can handle more effectively. This is a fatal mistake.

Every time you replace a "6" with a "9"

you have done a great service

for your company.

The reason some companies succeed when they are smaller is because, without realizing it, their ratio of nines to sixes is much higher, and the nines are in the key decision-making positions. A six will stand out in a group of nines in a small, dynamic company, and something will be done about it pretty quickly. However, as a company grows, it's easier for sixes to slip in; worse, they remain undetected. They can manipulate the company to their advantage, and they know how to play ball with other sixes. As a result, sixes attract other sixes while driving away nines because a nine will not work for a six very long. For any company, sixes are like a cancer that continues to grow. So, what can be done about it?

The problem is that most companies' employee evaluation systems are not designed to identify sixes easily. In my opinion, the best way to identify the top people in your organization is to force a key decision to be made by asking an employee's manager one simple question: Is John Jones a "nine" or a "six?" If John is not a six, the manager will almost always answer in one of two ways, either: "John's a nine," or, "Well, John's not really a nine, but he's a seven or an eight." However, if John is a six, a manager will always say, "John is a six," which may mean he is a five or a four. But the employee's manager will never give a rating of a seven or eight if the employee is a six.

Try it for yourself by asking any manager, and you will find that he or she can tell you in a few seconds who the nines are that report to him or her. Then, begin asking who are the sixes. Once you have the two groups of nines and sixes identified, you have won. By so doing, you will have done the single most important thing you could possibly do for your company.

Now the question is how to use this knowledge the most advantageously. First, compare your list with your company's organizational chart, and see how many nines and sixes are on that chart and where they fit in. A six should never be responsible for a major area of the company, and a six should never report to a six; sixes should always report to nines. A nine may be able to make a six function well through constant supervision and direction, but a six will always make another six worse, never better.

You should view every six on that chart as a blinking red light signaling you to do something about it now. The short-term solution is to restructure the organization so that nines control all responsible positions and that all sixes report directly to nines. Every time you replace a six with a nine, you have done a great thing for your company.

Most decisions in organizations are not complicated; rather, they are ones of common sense. The more people in the management structure with common sense (i.e., nines) means that their good judgment will be applied to day-to-day problems with outstanding long- and short-term results. Some people have difficulty understanding this concept of "nines" and "sixes." The key is how you ask a manager the question. It's very simple, actually. In fact, I recently discussed this issue with Joseph Tucci of Wang Laboratories, Inc., and he said, "I know what you mean. I call them empty suits."

MANAGEMENT INVOLVEMENT IN ADVERTISING

Given that a company's success depends on sales, what better way can a CEO spend his or her time than in figuring out how to increase sales by putting the competition on the defensive? A problem is that the president and senior management often leave this all-important function to others — the marketing or public relations departments or an advertising agency. Because developing a marketing campaign is a difficult, creative process, it's much easier for an executive just to ask the marketing department to do it, hope for some magic to happen and then criticize the results.

But, since most marketing people have never participated in direct sales, it is difficult for them to focus campaigns as effectively as they should. Consequently, it is far better for executive management to be truly involved in helping advertising and related media presentations reflect the company's competitive strengths. It will also help get the materials out much faster.

I am not suggesting dabbling in or interfering with the creative process, however. Rather, if senior management has up-front, heavy involvement with what the theme should be and how it should be communicated, it makes the job of the advertising, public relations and marketing people much easier. They can then creatively implement the theme and know that they are on target. Such involvement can drastically cut the wasted effort from idea to implementation. This will be a great competitive advantage in itself for any company.

> *Incorporate in your advertising*
>
> *what you find works well in personally*
>
> *selling prospects and customers.*

This is only possible if senior management constantly meets with clients and prospects (which they should be doing anyway). Simply translate what works in person into the promotional campaign. Also, realize that, in sales, the medium is often the message. Spend time and money ensuring that documentation, sales brochures, video presentations, advertising and demonstrations are outstanding and that they focus on benefits to the prospect. Otherwise, prospects will never become customers and find out how good your products really are.

Also, it is very important that company advertisements and promotional brochures are credible. This includes not only the themes but also the headlines, subtitles and body copy. A competitor or prospect ought to be able to read your advertisement and agree that it is an accurate and effective claim on your part. That alone will enhance your standing within the industry.

This involvement by senior management can, admittedly, drive advertising agencies and staff crazy. They feel it interferes with their creative responsibility. Nevertheless, when marketing departments and advertising agencies come back to you with suggested programs that are off the mark, and you have to tell them that, it is much worse for them and for you. The result is that money has been wasted and critical time has been lost while the positioning of your company and its products is slipping further and further behind. By not acting quickly, your company is doing its competitors a big favor.

ONE SENTENCE

Recently, I spoke with a new dean of a new school of a large university on how to develop his strategy for the future. The first thing I advised him to do was to define the role of the school in one sentence, so that everyone would understand the purpose and benefits of the school.

> *If you can't describe an idea*
>
> *in one sentence, you really*
>
> *don't understand the idea.*

I think he thought I hadn't understood the complexity of his school with its eleven institutes and centers. However, I had, and for years I had also spent many waking hours trying to understand complex, esoteric software products and reduce them to terms people would understand and would want to buy.

After agonizing over various new products for years, I developed a relatively simple method. It would go something like this at a meeting with the developers:

"We plan to run a full-page advertisement in a trade publication introducing this product, and it reads as follows:

Introducing Product X.

Now, you have one sentence to describe Product X in terms meaningful to a potential buyer."

If the developers or marketing people couldn't do it, it was clear they didn't understand the product and its real benefits. However, once this one sentence was arrived at, then it was easy to develop the advertising copy, brochures, slide presentations and related promotional material. Most important, everybody in the Company would now have a clear idea about the purpose of the product. Remember, a company's sales forces and other employees typically learn most about the company's products by what they read in the advertisements.

REVENUE FORECASTING

Most companies have great trouble with sales or revenue forecasting. Consequently, they have to live with a lot of unpleasant surprises that come when it is too late to do anything about them. It's bad enough to have poor sales in a quarter, but it's far worse to find out about it at the end of a quarter when you had been expecting good results, particularly if you are a publicly held company. This is inexcusable from a management point of view.

Fortunately, there is a fairly simple solution to unreliable forecasting. The problem is that most sales managers and salespeople don't forecast well. Their nature is to be overly optimistic in their estimates. They provide their management with the numbers they hope they will achieve rather than what are realistic. If you aren't careful, your company can go right off a cliff by operating at an expense level consistent with optimistic forecasts. This is deadly; yet, it happens all the time.

To get around this aspect of the "system," I used a very simple method for introducing great reliability into sales forecasting. For example, ask your vice president of sales to rate each of his or her regional manager's forecasting sales ability on a scale of 1 to 10, with a 1 representing 10% accuracy and a 10 representing 100% accuracy. If he or she normally delivers on 50% of what has been forecast, assign him or her a .50.

Then multiply each regional manager's forecast by his or her reliability factor to adjust their numbers to a more accurate prediction. When you have made this adjustment for every regional manager, add up the numbers. This becomes the company's sales forecast. Based on this forecast, it is now possible, with some degree of reliability, to plan expenses consistent with revenues.

Developing a sales reliability factor

will save you a lot of grief.

Let's say you have a $20 million revenue goal for a quarter, and forecasts predict $30 million, but the reliability factors, once applied, reduce the number to $20 million. Then you know that, while the company won't be producing the high revenues that were forecast, you are still in relatively good shape entering that quarter. On the other hand, if the "system" predicts $25 million and you need $20 million, and the reliability factors reduce the prediction to $18 million, then you know you're in trouble and you have to do something about it right away.

Knowing in time to do something about it is the critical benefit of this method. The hidden benefit of this method is that it saves you from listening to all the tedious details of each sales prospect, and then the post-mortems about why each didn't come about. It also gives you another way to surface the sixes. An individual's reliability factor will range, for example, from 40% to 90%. If a regional manager's or salesperson's track record is 50% or less, he or she doesn't really know what is happening with the prospects and, consequently, shouldn't be in this responsible position.

An individual's reliability factor is a great indicator of how good someone is at sales. I've always used it, and it has never let me down yet. Quite simply, if a manager has a track record of delivering on 60% of his forecasts in the past, why would anybody count on any more than 60% of his future forecasts? The really good people are at the 90% level.

Coping with the system demands such techniques from the CEO of a company. Otherwise, it will be too late to take corrective action. The CEO must find ways to assert a strong control over a fast-growing organization, or the "system" will eventually claim him as another victim.

THE PRESS & PUBLIC RELATIONS

I am not sure whether I or anyone else can provide a sure-fire method of communicating with the press. Nevertheless, there are at least three subsets of the press with which you should be concerned. They include your local newspapers, electronic media, magazines, etc.; the trade press; and the financial press.

The press and your interests

are not the same.

From an emotional point of view, the local media come first. It is where your neighbors, friends and acquaintances will read an article or see a television spot.

In a newspaper, for instance, an article may be positive, but the headline may be negative. This can happen because the person who writes an article often is not the one who writes the headline, which can be a great source of irritation if you or your company is the subject of the article.

On the subject of press and public relations, I have found that the following few guidelines work best:

1.   When somebody writes a negative story about you or your company, call the person. Rather than complain, ask him or her to lunch. Then at lunch, don't discuss the story, just get to know the person. Chances are, when the next article is written, you will be treated better.

2.   Return telephone calls. Since I try to do this with everybody, it never occurred to me how much people in the press appreciate it and how rarely it is done.

3.   Be honest.

4.   Don't have the same people who handle your public relations also handle your advertising. This angers the editorial staff of any publication. They are very sensitive about being pressured for coverage that is in any way related to advertising.

5.   Senior management should be available on a regular basis, particularly when there is important news, such as trouble. Don't let staff answer the questions in these situations. You won't like the results.

6.   Have your executives take the time to visit editors at their corporate headquarters once or twice a year. The editors appreciate it because it saves them travel time.

7.   When introducing a major product line, brief consultants in advance of your plans and answer their questions. The press often calls these people for their opinions after the press conference.

8.   Avoid press conferences. Instead, meet individually with the appropriate publications. They appreciate it very much because their individual questions are important to them.

9.   Try not to treat one publication more favorably than another. Be aware that daily, weekly and monthly publications have different deadlines. Make sure everybody gets the story in time to meet their own deadlines.

PUBLIC SPEAKING

Public speaking invitations are often full of surprises. For example, a customer once asked me to speak at a national computer conference to be held in Toronto. He said that Henry Kissinger was speaking on the first day, Tom Peters would be featured the second day, and I was to speak on the third day. I was impressed that I was included in such prestigious company and agreed to do it. The day before the speech, he called to say he was terribly embarrassed. He said if he had known what the conditions were, he would never have asked me to speak. It seems that the third day of the conference was the traditional "Vendor Day," and that the vendor paid for all the attendees' lunch. For this, the vendor got the opportunity to speak to the audience.

It was too late to back out. However, as I sat on the dais and watched 500 people eating at my expense, I fumed. When I asked the conference chairman how much Tom Peters received the previous day, he said, "$25,000." I gagged. I was giving a reasonable facsimile of a Tom Peters' speech and paying them to listen!

Some days, there is a free lunch.

Giving that speech was work. However, I suppose it was better than the time I drove to Yale to speak to the Yale Economic Forum. Unfortunately, it was the night before major exams, and no one showed up. I did get the opportunity to eat at Yale's famous eating club. That made it worth the trip.

Another speaking occasion of note was the day I spoke to an EDP Auditor's Group in San Diego. Located directly behind the Speaker's rostrum was the glass wall of an aquarium. Whenever I turned, I was eyeball-to-eyeball with some very large fish, who seemed content to just stare at me. It must have been disconcerting to the audience, but no one seemed to mind. Maybe they were used to it. I also got to say the Pledge of Allegiance there, something I had not done since grammar school.

Yet, probably nothing terrifies more executives than public speaking. I was no exception. However, over time and with much experience I have become much more than comfortable with a speaking assignment. In fact, this book is an extension of a talk by the same title I have given many times with excellent results.

My speaking guidelines are as follows:

1.   Make sure you are speaking on something you are knowledgeable about.

2.   Speak from notes, not from prepared text.

3.   Have the notes typed in the largest font size possible, such as 14 point, and number the pages in case you get them out of order.

4.   If you use slides or overheads, make sure the people in the back of the room can read the type. Never open a presentation with, "I don't know if the people in the back of the room can read this." Every time I have heard this comment, the people in the first row couldn't even read the words, let alone the people in the back. Include a copy of each slide at the appropriate place in your notes. This will allow you to avoid looking at the screen while you discuss a slide.

5.   Tailor the slides to the audience.

6.   Don't speak for more than 20 minutes. Get to the Q&A as soon as possible; people like to hear you answer their questions.

7.   Every 5-10 minutes make sure you introduce some humorous and related anecdote.

8.   Visit the room before you speak. Become familiar with the stage, the podium and the location of the mike. Run through the slides so that you are comfortable with the whole operation and your slides are in order, not upside down or missing, etc.

9.   If disaster befalls you, such as a power failure, have a humorous disaster story to tell. The audience will appreciate it.

10.   Call the person who asked you to speak, and ask about the audience. How many will be attending? What are their concerns? Who has spoken recently, and what was the topic? Never assume anything.

ENTERTAINING CLIENTS

How companies spend money, particularly in entertaining clients, is part of their culture. It has always fascinated me. For example, we have all attended elaborate and expensive functions held by corporations for clients and prospective clients. But what do they get for it? Does the amount of money spent determine the quality of the time? Of course not. I once witnessed an excellent example of how drastically different amounts of money were spent by two organizations; yet, both received excellent results.

The scene was at a bankers' trade show in Miami Beach, and two companies, both strong competitors for the banking industry's safe business, held cocktail parties for all attendees on subsequent nights. How these parties were organized tells a lot about how to spend money on customers. Company "X" was very rich. Company "Y" wasn't and couldn't match its competitor's resources.

Company X held a beautiful cocktail party. They had 3,000 people attend and spared no expense to show the people a class time. It was enjoyable, the food was expensive and terrific, and it was a successful party. I went out of there feeling, if I were a banker, there was no doubt that I would buy an X Company safe. Company Y didn't stand a chance.

The next night, Y held a much less expensive event at which they served just wine, beer, cheese and crackers. It wasn't nearly as elegant as X's party had been, and not quite as many people attended. However, the company did something unique. They had a band and passed out song books and encouraged people to participate in a regional sing-along. People sang songs representing their home states, and it became a very competitive and truly enjoyable event.

This simple approach "involved" the attendees, and they appreciated it enormously. In addition, the Company Y's people participated in the sing-along, creating a bond with clients and prospects that was special and lasted into the next day and beyond. Long after, people were still feeling good about the party and about Company Y — not bad for an event that probably cost only a tenth of X's party, and it was much more fun. If I were a banker thinking about buying a safe, Company Y was going to get serious consideration.

More is not necessarily better.

It is almost a law that, the more money that you spend on some corporate extravaganza, the less enjoyable it will be. One of the reasons is that it will be overproduced and lack spontaneity. Successful companies, however, eventually find many ways to spend serious money, including the corporate headquarters. Whenever a "successful" company begins to plan a corporate "campus" or has a waterfall in its reception area, watch out. Trouble may be just down the road.

ON SALES PEOPLE

Hiring and retaining salespeople with the right qualities is a critical task for senior management. A good salesperson will generate ten times the business of a poor one. Poor ones can actually defoliate a territory. What does senior management do that is so important that they can't spend more time on this issue?

When a salesperson walks into the office of a customer or a potential customer, he or she *is* the company. That's what the client sees, not the corporate headquarters back home.

Like most companies, the Company held a yearly quota club meeting of its most successful salespeople. The club honored those who had reached or exceeded their quota. The first meeting I attended, I was struck by how different these successful salespeople were. Some were tall, others were short, some were handsome, others not so. Almost no one fit into the classic "IBM stereotype" of what we think a salesperson should look like. They did not share any common physical denominator. Their personalities were also quite different. Yet, they were all very successful at selling the Company's software.

People buy things

from people they like and respect.

Then, what makes salespeople successful? This is an issue with which anyone involved in sales wrestles, continuously. After 25 years in sales and sales management, I have reduced the issue to one sentence: "People buy things from people they like and respect." That's the common denominator. Moreover, people like and respect people for a number of reasons, and it has very little to do with an individual's physical characteristics or personality.

Prospective clients like salespeople who care enough about them to learn about their problems, yet don't waste their time and don't oversell. However, prospects respect good salesmanship and understand that a salesperson's job is to get the business. Nevertheless, they don't like getting second-rate treatment; in fact, they resent it.

The most important quality a salesperson can possess is empathy, an ability to look at a prospect's problem from his or her point of view. With empathy, he or she can build a relationship with a client, which is the basis of all successful sales efforts. Without empathy, a salesperson will flounder and wonder why he or she is not more effective. They have this his certain blind spot that no training will change. This is why good salespeople are born and not made.

Senior management should spend much more time interviewing sales and sales management candidates than they do. The candidates actually appreciate the fact that you consider their function so important that you will take the time to interview them.

SALES AWARENESS PLAN

All of us have at one time or another called some organization, only to be directed to the wrong department and then treated poorly by some non-caring employee. The experience turns us off on the organization. On the other hand, we are particularly impressed when we receive good treatment in such situations. It is a true indication of a well-run company.

Everyone likes

to be considered important.

When the Company was small, a sale was so critical to our survival that we couldn't afford to lose a single one, certainly not because some employee was too casual or even rude to a prospect calling in for the first time. To avoid this problem, we instituted the Sales Awareness Plan. This plan had an incentive for every employee, indicating that the Company was willing to pay for good and responsive service at every level of the organization. Specifically, we put a percentage of every sale into a pool that was divided equally among all employees each quarter. The key was "equality."

For example, we had people in the shipping department who were making $10,000 per year who now were getting an extra $800 per quarter, the same amount as the Senior Vice President of Technical Development. I once was in the shipping department and noticed a calendar on the wall with Xs on all the dates up to one date. I asked the shipping clerk the meaning of the Xs. He said that they indicated the number of days left before the Sales Awareness Plan bonus was paid. It was like "found" money to most employees. This is what they used to buy new stereos or take a vacation, etc.

I was astounded at the popularity of the plan. Most importantly, the plan said as clearly as possible to all employees that the Company considered everyone equally important, regardless of their position, and that service was key to the Company's method of operation.

ABOUT DEMONSTRATIONS & PRESENTATIONS

Demonstrations in the computer business, or any business, are always fraught with potential peril. Simplicity and brevity can help avoid disaster and help win over a busy prospect. One particular demonstration, held in a plush Atlanta dining room, of a halon-based fire suppression system designed to protect computer facilities from fire disasters is a classic example of a complicated demonstration gone awry.

The key benefit of halon is that it puts out fires without asphyxiating the people in the room at the time. It is like a fog that doesn't damage clothes or equipment in the process. To demonstrate the halon, the vendor put a glass-walled telephone booth in the middle of the dining ring room and lit candles inside the booth. The conference chairman volunteered to stand inside the booth, wearing his new suit, to demonstrate how the product would put out the candle flames without hurting him or damaging his suit. Right on schedule, a fog filled the booth, and he quickly disappeared. Then we heard a loud explosion. Eventually, we could make out his face staring out of the booth in terror. No one knew what had happened, but we all seemed to look up at the same time to a big, gaping hole in the ceiling where bent girders had been exposed.

What happened was that the canister of halon, which was shaped like a bomb and had been bolted inside the booth, had ripped itself out and had taken off like a rocket. Fortunately, it went straight up instead of sideways, or half of us would have been killed. This had to be the worse demonstration I have ever seen, in an industry that is famous for bad demonstrations.

Recently, by chance, I met with the man who was ultimately in charge of the salesperson who had conducted the demonstration. He had never heard of the episode. I wondered how his company had paid for that big hole in the dining room ceiling without his knowing about it. However, this only proves my point made earlier about communication from a salesperson in the field to the vice president of marketing. Rarely does the true story get through the layers of management.

I clearly remember another presentation, one that the Company made to the Strategic Air Command Headquarters (SAC) in Omaha, Nebraska. We were a small company then, and SAC was seriously considering using our database software for some important applications. They had asked me to come out to Omaha and make a presentation to General Robert Evans, who was in charge of all information systems for SAC.

I was delighted to do this, of course, and traveled to Omaha to meet with him. An assistant to the General met me at the gate. He said to me, "Before you give your presentation to the General, I have a presentation to give to you on how we plan to use your database software."

He proceeded with an elegant 35mm slide show, illustrating that the Company's software was going to control all the sorties of the B-52 nuclear-carrying capacity of the United States worldwide, all missions of the U2 and SR71 spy flights worldwide and the action or reaction of the United States versus Russia, etc.

"My God," I thought. "The first line of defense of the United States is going to be controlled by my software." I hadn't planned on that! As I went in to meet the general, my knees were shaking, and I could hear the "Star Spangled Banner" playing in my head. Then I looked down the long table of grim-looking colonels, bedecked in all their battle ribbons, and a dour general down at the end of the table.

As I was about to get under way with my presentation, General Evans interrupted me in a gruff way and said, "Look, if your software doesn't work, now is the time to admit it and get the hell out of here!" If it didn't, I surely would have felt obliged to do so. It would have been my patriotic duty. But since our software worked well, I pressed on.

However, before I got going, I held up my 35mm slide projector carousel, which was full of slides. The colonels, like any group that is about to be assaulted with a long and possibly very tedious presentation, eyed the carousel to gauge the length of the presentation. They were thinking, as we would all do in this situation, "How long is this presentation going to be?" I said, "See all these slides?" I paused and then said, "Well, I'm only going to use five of them!" They broke into spontaneous applause of appreciation and relief.

In any presentation, less is better.

I always wince when a salesperson boasts about how long he or she spent with a prospect. I know we'll never get the business. As in the presentation to SAC, less is better. For one thing, it forces you to think about what is really important. More importantly, your prospect will appreciate your concern for his or her time.

KNOWLEDGE

Learning something new is a great experience, and everything I have ever learned, however obscure, proved to be of significant value at some late date. One negative in building a successful company is that you often have to solve the same problem over and over again. While corporate survival may demand it, and you may be very good at it, the result may be that you wind up with a much more limited knowledge span and sources of advice than you realize. In other words, you may have ten years' experience, but in reality you may have one year's experience ten times. This is the way I felt after I had sold the Company. Only in my case, I had worked for four new ventures over thirty years, solving exactly the same problems.

Consequently, when I had the opportunity to become a Fellow in the Center for Business and Government at the John F. Kennedy School of Government at Harvard University, I jumped

at it. Besides, my newest great learning experience – trying to
play a few simple tunes on the piano – was driving my wife to
distraction.

The Center for Business and Government, under the direction of Professor John Dunlop, was to hold some surprises for
me – all positive. First, the Center's economists weren't aca-
demic stereotypes. They were intensively involved in solving
major problems facing countries around the world, including
our own. In some cases, they were on the Boards of Directors of
important corporations and were intimately familiar with the
executive decision-making process. Professor John Meyer, in
his "Mergers & Acquisitions" class was particularly astute at
introducing the human element in executive decision making.
My experience is that most managers and students have a very
difficult time comprehending that a president of a company
might locate a new plant or office at a site whose main and only
redeeming feature is that it happens to be located close to a
favorite golf course of ski resort.

Make the time to learn.

At a place like the Center, a person's assumptions are chal-
lenged completely. Leading scholars from around the world
present papers every Thursday on a wide range of topics and
are quizzed on the paper by the Center's faculty. I love to sit
and listen to the discussions. It's a very fast league. We spend
so much time watching professional athletes perform in America that it's a pleasure to watch great professional minds in
action.

The problem is that so many executives like me don't take
the time when they are running their companies to learn and
meet new people. If I had to do it all over again, I would force
myself into such a learning situation or take a Sabbatical. I
think it would have been very good for my company, particularly as it became very big. At the least, I could have learned
about "harvest" strategies, which is how to get out of a successful
venture and when. Then, again, they weren't talking about harvest strategies back then.

DECISIONS

As a CEO of your company, you will make many good decisions and some mistakes that will make you wonder how you could have been so stupid. Most CEOs don't mind admitting these mistakes over cocktails at some industry conference. It's almost a "Can you top this?" exercise. It is also quite therapeutic. Frankly, it's more important to admit to mistakes back at the company — and the sooner, the better. For example, when you have promoted someone into a new job or are pursuing some strategy that turns out to be wrong, move quickly to rectify it. Willingness of executive management to admit their mistakes and do something about them is very good for a company's culture. It's also good for the business. My view is that a CEO is making decisions all day long and, thus, statistically destined to make mistakes. However, a CEO gets paid to make the important decisions right.

> *An expression rarely heard at decision time in American corporations is, "This idea is really dumb."*

One technique that seemed to work exceptionally well for me was to listen to knowledgeable staff with divergent views debate what the Company should do regarding some complex technical issue. As the debate wore on, it would often become obvious to me what the Company should do. I would further test this conclusion by having our top people discuss their position with selected clients or prospects that I felt had a particularly strong sense of which technology was going to be critical to their companies in the future. You would be amazed at how quickly the tone of the debate changes, once you have introduced prospects and customers into the process. Customer requirements that were ridiculed in the staff meeting have a way of becoming very legitimate once the customer has had a chance to explain his or her real needs. Once this critical test of our position had been made, I felt pretty confident that we were on the right track.

An interesting note here is that this approach worked exceedingly well during the 1970s, when we were smaller and it was easier to do. Also, the Company was blessed with a cadre of very bright, highly opinionated individuals with very strong technical backgrounds, who spent a lot of their time on the front lines, selling and installing the Company's products. They knew what they were talking about, and they weren't shy about telling me or anyone else when they thought that the Company was doing something dumb, an invaluable contribution to a fast-growing company. Since I respected them and their knowledge, we rarely had any problems. I also liked the meetings because I knew that this was an unparalleled group of database experts and that the Company was a technical powerhouse because of them.

INTERNATIONAL CONNECTIONS

At first, the Company operated overseas through agents or consulting firms. My first visit to Europe came after Jurgen Schoon began representing Cullinane products in Germany. He set up a meeting near Bremen with VF Fokker, his first client for our products. During my introduction to our client, I used a few German words I had learned, and his response was, "Ah! You speak German! Most Americans don't. How can they expect to do business with us?" I was in a very awkward situation, and it pointed out to me the importance of learning foreign languages, which, incidentally, are not foreign in someone else's country.

People are the same around the world.

Later, I set up our own subsidiaries, a move welcomed by prospects and customers; it meant that we were serious about their business. The first was in Belgium and covered Belgium and the Netherlands. Through the efforts of Jan Herremans, Jan Picavet and others, it was spectacularly successful in outselling IBM and other competitors.

In dealing with colleagues from other countries, I have found that they have the same interests as we — family, success at their jobs, a love of music and so many other things. However, their cultures may be thousands of years older than ours, and they may have developed a far more subtle or sophisticated style of negotiation. This can be compounded by the fact that they may not be fluent in English, and it requires that you learn to listen that much more carefully to what they are saying in order to get a sense of what they are really driving at. You have to really concentrate at it.

Finally, foreigners are no different from us in that they like to do business with people they trust. Distance and the differences in languages make trust that much more important in any international relationship. Frankly, I found that the style I found effective in the United States worked equally well in other countries.

SIX THINGS I WOULD RECOMMEND THAT ANY MANAGER DO

Every manager should take a sales training course.

---

1. Take a sales training course. Sales is a skill every manager or CEO should learn, and few do. Not until you have taken a sales training course will you realize how little you know about sales.

2. Read history. Everything that is happening to you or your company has already happened a million times to others.

3. Learn to listen. You never learn anything while you're talking; ask open-ended questions, such as who, what, when, where and how, and then listen to the response.

4. Drop in on meetings of your staff. It's amazing what you will find out, including a lot of things you will never hear at your staff meetings.

5. When you're in a meeting of your peers and their management and something that bothers you is being promoted in a rational way, listen for your concerns to be resolved. If they are not resolved by the time the discussion is coming to a close, raise your hand and mention what bothers you about the discussion.

6. Try to learn to think like your company's CEO by looking at your company from his or her perspective. Your CEO will find this remarkably rare and refreshing.

Chapter Eight

Management Style

Discussing one's management style is not easy to do. One reason is that I have a tendency to make it look and sound easy, and it isn't. However, it is important to note that your management style might be quite different than mine but just as effective. There is no "one" style. When I formed the Company, there were no books to read or guidelines to follow and, for that matter, no software industry in existence. I just developed a sense of what to do at a particular time because it "felt right" or because common sense dictated it.

Make the tough decisions.

A sure indication that a problem was critical was my waking up at 4 a.m. thinking about it, which led one non-admirer of my style to once comment that I ran the Company based on the way I got out of bed in the morning — a very astute observation. The solution to the problem often involved the necessity of calling to task someone who wasn't doing his or her job. If I were waking up at 4, I knew the problem couldn't be ignored any longer and that something had to be done. I felt I owed it to the people who *were* doing a good job to protect them and the Company from those who weren't.

MANAGING ORGANIZATION & CHANGE

Attempts to structure management responsibilities according to a nice, neat organizational chart never seemed to work. The organization always wanted to work differently than the way I originally envisaged. From experience, I learned to structure the management organization according to how the system wants to work and how it works best. This may result in some odd reporting arrangements and responsibilities, but don't worry about it. Keep changing them as the needs change.

Organize the way

the system wants to work.

Companies, in particular, hate change. Be an "agent of change;" otherwise, your company will atrophy. Keep one foot in tomorrow and one in today even though, at times, your staff may not like it. Someone has to play this all-important role, and many times you will have to force the issue. An idea today may turn into the savior of tomorrow. But when it happens, don't expect anyone to remember that it was your idea to pursue this new activity in the first place.

ROLE RUTS & SKILLS

I have always been fascinated by people and how they get typecast in certain positions for no good reason. One lasting impression of *Up the Organization*, Townsend's sacrilegious but invaluable book on corporate America, was how Townsend was told when he took over AVIS that there was no management depth and the first thing he would have to do would be to hire a new management team. Well, he looked around and found that AVIS already had a lot of potential talent; no one had taken the time to acknowledge it in the past.

It is cheaper and better to promote people who know your company and have a proven track record. As a manager, that's what you have to do. If you are continually impressed at how efficient and committed an employee of your company is, regardless of the job, think about that commitment in another, more important position, and give the employee a chance to grow into it. You will be amazed at the results after six months.

Each manager has different skills. A manager ought to be given only that amount of rope that person can accommodate. If your managers have weaknesses, it is up to you to balance those weaknesses yourself or through some other support mechanism. They, and you, will have to change your responsibilities as a company grows; otherwise, it will strangle your company in the future.

> *Talent is in the eye of the beholder.*

You and your managers will have to do this in order to get through the traditional entrepreneurial barriers of 25, 50, 100, 200, etc. people in place. Each barrier requires that the entrepreneur give up some responsibility and rely more on other people. Many entrepreneurs have great difficulty with this issue, and their companies suffer accordingly.

[TOWNSEND70]   Robert Townsend. *Up the Organization*, 1st Edition, Knopf, New York, 1970.

SOUNDING BOARDS

A lot of people are sources of important advice about what to do or where the company should be going. Ironically, these people reporting to you are often not the best sources of input. They may, without realizing it, want to keep you "happy." Another reason may be that major changes would often impact their sphere of influence of the organization.

One sounding board is your employees – at all levels. Seek them out in informal settings, such as the company cafeteria.

Listen to your employees.

Employees are great sources of input, particularly if you listen carefully.

CONTROL TOWER VS. THE COCKPIT

When my Company was starting up, I didn't like to fly, and I didn't want to be away from home on long trips. Consequently, the control-tower approach to management was more my style. This resulted in the encouragement of strong regional managers and heads of our subsidiaries. They were "presidents" of mini-companies, with whom I would talk over the telephone but rarely visit.

The positive side of this style was that I was always available and accessible to calls from the field, customers or prospects. I know that, because of this, I was able to catch many, many problems in time to do something before they became fatal. It might have meant responding to some important prospect in time to keep from losing a sale to innumerable other problems.

There is no "one" way to manage.

In addition, we encouraged executives of prospects to come to Boston for meetings with key members of the Company's executive team or presentations by me on topics they might find timely, such as "Information Systems Strategies for the '80s and '90s." This saved us the trouble of traveling to their offices and were most effective in closing major contracts.

There was a time when we had as many as ten companies a day visiting, and I and other members of executive management would drop in on all ten. We always served sandwiches for lunch, and I don't think I ate much else for lunch for years; however, the result was that we sold about 95 per cent of those that came to our offices.

The control-tower approach does have its negatives. For example, the reason we were strong in the United States and Europe was that I had met some of our key prospective employees on my trips and had created offices and subsidiaries with them. We had no presence in the Far East, and I believe it was due to the fact that I had never visited that part of the world. However, when you look at the control-tower approach to management, you can be a positive factor in perhaps 100 key items per week by being in the office, while being on the road you might address only 20.

ANTICIPATE

Much of my time at the Company was spent anticipating problems in order to prevent them. This meant always looking at systems or series of steps with an eye for weak links in the chain. One method was to try to think like a customer and interact with the process or product as an outsider to see where it might break down. It often did, and the bigger the event and the more people involved, the higher became the probability of a major potential flaw in the system. Troubleshooting from the inside saved a lot of trouble from the outside.

On a more mundane level, if by three in the afternoon, you are feeling pretty good that you have caught everything regarding a company event due to start at six, make sure that you drop by at 5:30 just to check. More likely than not, an X factor will have been introduced in the interim that could turn your very important event into a disaster. Almost always, some well intentioned change will require a flurry of action to correct at the last moment.

HAPPINESS

When people asked me what business I was in, I would tell them, "the happiness business." My job was to keep customers, employees and investors happy, and customers came first.

If I received a letter from an irate client, I would immediately call the person, who would often be shocked that the CEO of a major software firm would call him or her personally. I would explain that my purpose was to acknowledge the letter and to assure that I would follow through with a response. I would then call Gary Wright, the Company's head of Support. After determining what the facts were, he would develop a plan to solve the problem and then contact the customer. A few days later, I would again call the customer to find out if things were happening to his or her satisfaction. They usually were.

These problems were incredibly complex, and solving them was not an easy task. Often I would receive a call from a customer some time later and groan, thinking that, perhaps, the problem had not been solved and that the customer was still upset. Invariably, however, the customer was calling to thank me for the great job that the Company's staff had done. This process turned a lot of potential enemies into loyal friends who gave us great references or, when they moved on to new jobs, bought the Company's software again.

> *It is the responsibility of the CEO*
>
> *to keep customers happy.*

Once, at a User Group meeting in Athens, it was brought to my attention that the French users were very unhappy. So, I invited them to my suite to listen to their complaints firsthand. After a short while, it was obvious they had a very legitimate gripe. The Company was being represented in France by a consulting firm. When its support people became skilled in our Company's products, the representing company turned them into billable consultants, leaving the users without support.

I committed to open a French subsidiary of the Company within six months and staff it with top technical talent from the United States, which we did. The first person assigned was Troy Rudolph. The day he was leaving for Paris, I received a telex from the Barcelona Stock Exchange, complaining that the Company's software was causing them major problems and had for months. It was a serious situation. I caught Troy in time to ask that he continue on from Paris to Barcelona to find out what their problem was. In one day, he determined that the problem was with IBM's software, and it was resolved quickly.

By the way, the previously disgruntled French users sent a bottle of champagne to my table after our meeting.

Of course, there are limits. One busy Friday I received ten telephone calls from one customer at a site where the Company was conducting a training course for a number of clients and he was the host. In the last one, which came about 5 p.m., his complaint was that there had been no jelly doughnuts during the coffee breaks. If you want to know what my breaking point is in good customer relations, that's it.

ON STAYING ALIVE

Most executives come face to face with their mortality at about 30. Usually it is a result of having done some heavy lifting over their heads. The morning after, they wake up with severe pain across their chests, which they think might be a heart attack when, in reality, it is just a case of strained muscles. I know. It happened to me.

A more serious case occurred when I had been in a stressful work situation for some time, ate something that didn't agree with me, and threw up violently. Out came blood. The bathroom started to spin, and eventually I was carted off to the hospital in an ambulance. It turned out to be nothing. In fact, I was embarrassed to be in the hospital. Subsequently, I learned that Bill Russell, the great Boston Celtics basketball player, often did this before important games and that the same thing had happened to President Bush when he was about thirty; only he had an ulcer.

The experience had a lasting impact on me, namely, that success wasn't worth sacrificing one's health. Thereafter, with the knowledge that I had a stomach that could take only so much abuse, I tried to balance my activities. For example, the best way for me to get into trouble is to engage in two weeks of non-stop breakfast, lunch and dinner meetings, including cocktail parties with rich food — compounded by stressful days filled with many deadlines, speeches, trips or important decisions.

Listen to your system.

Some executives add smoking, coffee and high-tension competitive golf or tennis matches on weekends and then wonder why they have trouble. Inevitably, any system will start to rebel. Every doctor will tell you that you know your system better than anyone else and that you had better listen to it.

ON BEING A V.I.P.

On occasion, a founder of a successful company will become a V.I.P. In fact, creators of successful personal-computer software products have often been referred to as "rock stars," they have become so well known. My brushes with V.I.P. status would come, primarily, at User Weeks. When your company is responsible for bringing four or five thousand people to a city for a week, you get V.I.P. status.

You first become aware of it when you notice billboards on the highway from the host city airport welcoming you and your company. Once, approaching the hotel hosting User Week in Las Vegas I could see "Cullinane" in huge letters on its sign, giving me top billing with Steve Lawrence and Eydie Gorme. The cab driver then said, "Whose this Cullinane?" and I said, "That's me!" with a certain satisfaction. After all, how many times do you get your name in lights in Las Vegas? The cab driver turned and stared at me to see if I were telling the truth, and I'll never know if he believed me.

I didn't care; it was all heady stuff. Under huge banners featuring "Cullinane" I was whisked past the long registration lines and up to the most expensive suite in the hotel, provided gratis to V.I.Ps.

Importance is in the eye of the beholder.

The color scheme of lime green wasn't exactly my taste, nor was the bed. And the mirror on the ceiling didn't bother me, either. What did was that the bed was situated on a pedestal — a serious lapse in interior decorating logic. If you got up in the middle of the night, you could break your neck falling down the stairs.

The Company's User Week begins on Sunday and closes on Thursday. Curiously, by Tuesday night, I began to notice my name disappearing from the signs. I was devolving into non-person status just as I was beginning to enjoy the fame. By Wednesday, my name was no longer up in lights on the Great White Way. By the time I checked out, I was a nobody again.

As anybody who has been a V.I.P. for a day or more knows, fame is fleeting. This particularly hits home when, after a busy day and nothing to eat, the V.I.P. ends up at some dreary lunch counter, eating a grungy hot dog in a deserted airport where nobody knows or cares who you are.

THE FOUNDER'S DILEMMA

The founder of a very successful firm faces a dilemma. What does he or she do for a long-term career path? For example, the founder can stay around for so long that there is an inevitable, sad or bitter parting of the ways. It happened in the case of Edwin Land, Founder of the Polaroid Corporations, one of the great entrepreneurs and scientists of our age.

Mitch Kapor, Founder of Lotus Development Corporation, took another approach. He saw his great success as a "jail." He simply resigned, turned Lotus over to Jim Manzi and sold all his stock. He is now still young, wealthy and free of any responsibility for Lotus' results. Consequently, he is able to devote his time to activities of personal interest, such as computer crime legislation. I suspect he is working as hard as ever but in different arenas.

Another solution is to intentionally paint yourself out of the picture. This means bringing along a management team by gradually turning over responsibility for the corporation to them. It includes eventually appointing one of them as President, with the intent of leaving completely, once the new president has proven him- or herself capable of running the company. This was my approach.

The last option would be continue to run the company the way you always have, with the assumption that there are going to be ups and downs along the way. Good people will leave because they will see their career paths blocked. You will take a lot of "heat" for this, but the alternative is that you, the Founder, will have to leave to accommodate them, not necessarily a good trade. Up until his recent retirement, Ken Olsen of Digital was the best example I know of this school.

Frankly, in 1983, when I appointed a new president, I thought seriously about leaving completely. I knew I should do it, but maybe being Chairman of the Board was too nice a deal to give up so easily. I kept postponing leaving until, finally, we had the inevitable down quarter, and I was stuck.

> *Somebody has to be in charge.*

As you begin to share responsibility in an entrepreneurial venture while you paint yourself out of the picture, it confuses people. Who is really running the company? You used to be President, and now someone else is. I am sure it doesn't make the new president's job any easier, either.

You are either running a company or not. To me, it is a most important distinction. The best way I can describe the former is that you feel a personal responsibility for the company, wake up at four in the morning thinking about its problems and then make sure that the solutions are implemented properly. There is no doubt about who's in charge or that second-class performance will not be tolerated.

Great organizations always have someone at the top who sets high performance standards and insists that they be met. At this point, let me hasten to add that most employees want to work for a company with an outstanding reputation and don't like it when some fellow employee is not holding up his or her end.

Chapter Nine

Creating the Corporate Culture

CORPORATE CULTURE

It is an inescapable fact of corporate life that the leader sets the tone and strongly influences the culture of a company, from the executive offices to the shipping dock. The ethics of the CEO ripple down through the organization and are seen and felt in the branches and elsewhere.

The question I have often been asked is, "Which is more important, the official or the unofficial corporate culture?" The answer is obvious: Your employees will do what you do and not what you say. Then again, maybe it isn't so obvious.

> *The leader establishes the culture.*

When my son was small, I would tell him to do something a certain way, and sometimes he wouldn't. Well, I puzzled over this for a long time. Why doesn't he do something the way I tell him to? Then it dawned on me. He wasn't doing things the way I said to do them; he was doing things the way I did them. All of us view ourselves in terms of our best behavior. We forget that we have lapses and often don't practice what we preach.

A corporate culture is just like a family. The president or leader establishes by his or her own code of ethics how the company is really going to function.

The employees watch closely and will take their lead from the president; so, every corporate executive should do some soul-searching on this issue. Every time you cut a corner or refuse to acknowledge a problem, this will be part of the culture that will spread throughout the company.

A Personal View: Jon Nackerud

Getting Acquainted

Immediately upon being employed at the Company, I was scheduled to attend a database installation and training class. Since most new hires were already experienced with the products, qualifying as a trainer required little more than attending a class. One such class was being taught in Canada the next Monday by a fellow employee who was highly regarded and experienced.

Sunday night, as I checked in at the hotel, I was handed a message marked "urgent." It was from that same colleague, and I phoned him when I got to my room. It was his first week with the Company, and he hadn't a clue what the class was about, let alone teach it. He panicked. Sensing the irony of this situation, I asked him what he had been told about me. It seems I had been described to him as an experienced trainer, one of the best! Assuring him I'd see him in the morning, I unpacked the manuals, read through them and worked on a lesson plan until early the next morning. Total immersion. Sink or swim.

Thinking about it, I was excited, amused and happy. I taught the class, and it got very positive reviews by the class members and my fellow employee. About a month later, he left the company. From that day on, whenever I interviewed a person to work for our Company, I told them this story and asked for their comments. They never knew it, but their response was the most important part of the interview.

The Six-Second Company Procedure Manual

About a month after I started at the Company, I reluctantly asked John Cullinane to describe my duties, my "charter." After a brief chuckle, he said it was simple — just do everything as well as he did or better. To this day I have not heard a more elegant or complete way to describe corporate conduct. Fortunately, it was delivered by a model of propriety, civility, decency and business judgment. Good leaders make good companies.

Company Culture 101

Absorbing the corporate culture from the field is often difficult. At the Company, the grapevine always worked, and stories that contributed to the culture of the Company were passed along rapidly — but were often distorted by the time they got to the west coast.

One such story emphasizes the Company policy that "the customer comes first." It seems Employee X was stopped for speeding while on the way to make a presentation at a prospect site. The police discovered that X had outstanding traffic warrants and put him in jail. He needed to be bailed out and called John Cullinane to explain the circumstances. "Did you call the prospect first and explain that you would be delayed?" "No." "Then you're fired." Over the years I learned that this was not exactly what transpired, but in the field, it became Gospel.

Another circulating story involved a salesman who treated himself well at Company expense. Any salesman accompanied by a freshly signed contract was welcome to fly home first class. It so happened that he was in first class when John Cullinane boarded the plane and sat in coach. John stopped to chat with Y and told him he was pleased that he had made a sale and was looking forward to hearing more about it the next day at the office. The next day, no contract led to no job. Some of us weren't too sorry for him as he had been one of those people who had shown a lack of judgment while in the field. I had been asked to bring those transgressions to the attention of the home office but didn't feel it was necessary. If he screwed up in the field, I was sure he'd screw up at home, and it would be taken care of. The plane episode happened so soon thereafter that it seemed like magic.

The Story of the Nines

I separated from the Company but rejoined after a few years to help reverse its decline. In the past, we had used the term "a nine" to refer to any employee who was self-motivated, self-managed, trustworthy, reliant, competent, etc. We had worked hard to make the Company a team of nines and had diligently pruned out those who didn't measure up. Upon my return, there were many problems, but the most shocking was the small percentage of nines. What had happened?

Soon after, I passed on to John Cullinane a story I had read about an entrepreneur who had left his company only to see it performing so poorly after two years that he had to return to save it. The man had described his problem as "a loss of nines." He said that, when he left, it was a company of "nines," but they had made the mistake of hiring "eights." The "eights" had hired "sevens," and so on. When he returned, the average employee was about a "six." He said that if he could get it back to a company of nines, all his problems would be solved.

Not all good stories have happy endings. Maybe that is what happened to the Company. It takes a strong person to work with people who are as good or better than they are. Perhaps managers think their chances for advancement are better if they surround themselves with "lesser" coworkers. The damage to the Company resulting from this problem was not irreversible, but we did not have the time to fix it. Customers had lost confidence in the Company and its products. The money was running out. The old gave way to the new. We had lost. It was a tragedy.

I can say, though, that for years I had worked with the best people for the best company in the world.

A Personal View: Bill Casey

Without doubt, each participant in the Company's success story carried around his or her own rationale for what made it happen in the 1970s. It was not due to our line of business. Similarly, it was not merely the collection of intelligent and ambitious individuals that made the organization unique. "Smart" people are good to have around, but many firms capitalizing only on brightness fail annually. At Cullinane, there was a definite corporate culture, and many of us unwittingly built it.

We thrived on building outstanding products, enjoyed meeting — and exceeding — customer expectations, and conducted business the way we felt it should be conducted. While we were moderately well paid, none of us was there simply because of the money. We were there because we wanted to be there.

In 1976, a prospective employee remarked, "Cullinane Corporation is the fastest track." None of us thought of it as such. We thought of it as a place where we liked working with each other and shared the effort and accomplishment that comes with a successful team endeavor.

In my opinion, the most important factor in our growth was our ability and willingness, as a matter of standard procedure, to fire personnel. This was not an obtuse policy; rather, it derived from a leanly-construed organization that depended on each person carrying more than his or her weight in the sales force, in field support or in development. Regardless of a new employee's record of accomplishments elsewhere, once on board at Cullinane, he or she had to be contributing in a relatively short timeframe. Within one or two months, many new employees were fully functional, and virtually all achieved this level within a half-year. Those who did not were gone.

Mistakes will be made and are unavoidable. The job "filled" by a person is never exactly as outlined before hire, nor is the person sitting across the table during the screening process quite the same one on the payroll two or three weeks later. In a young company growing as rapidly as we were, many people were hired based on their perceived potential. Few came to us with large amounts of relevant experience. Surprisingly, prior experience occasionally served as a serious obstacle rather than as an aid to new employees. For some, a disinclination to relearn a different system — our IDMS — from the ground up proved a permanent impediment.

Educational credentials and track record were not especially useful; we expected new employees to take advantage of a rough mentoring system and learn on the job. Inability to deal with customers was one frequent difficulty, particularly for new hires used to operating in a "customer" as opposed to a vendor environment. Immaturity travels in many guises, but a person who failed to project a serious and professional interest in and concern for the customer's problems had no place at Cullinane.

We not only sought to hire the best talent we could find, but there was never a reluctance to hire people who were "better." The most notorious company story of this sort involves Bob Goldman, hired by Ron McKinney and Tom Meurer in Cleveland in late 1973 as an IDMS programmer. Within two years, Bob had become Ron's boss in development and subsequently rose to become President of the Company. Variations on this theme occurred in many other instances. It was virtually unheard of for people to leave Cullinane because they were placed under anyone, even a person they had hired.

One good person could be as effective as half a dozen "regular" employees. What was one Tom Nelson worth? Unassuming Tom was brought to Cullinane through my efforts in 1974 and served as the indispensable Godfather of the Company's software architecture well into the 1980s. He envisioned and oversaw the evolution of IDMS from a simple, well-constructed data management facility to a modern high-volume on-line production system that outperformed anything else available. Hiring 100 technicians would not have provided Cullinane as much benefit as Tom Nelson alone.

Symptomatically, turnover among key personnel was insignificant during the 1970s. That stability itself, which allowed the addition of new contributors but was not characterized by erosion of talent became an important part of the Cullinane strength.

Family Considerations

Surprisingly, few of the core group of people at Cullinane during the mid-1970s would be described as workaholics. Though we all worked very hard long days, the atmosphere was not one of work as an all-inclusive priority. A mindset shared by all recognized family as important, and this mindset definitely came from the top. John Cullinane saw these as matters of consequence, so it was easy for most of us to do so as well.

On my first day at the Company, in 1973, John did not arrive in the office until after lunch. After seeing a client, he had stopped to visit his mother. This always stuck in my mind as being both admirable and unusual. Internal pressures to continuously be at work during periods of fast growth of a corporation were tempered in the Cullinane atmosphere.

Of course, there was considerable travel for many of us. The problem was especially acute in 1975-76, when the Company had achieved considerable success but was still in the process of establishing functional field offices around the country and overseas. As a result, many of us came under domestic pressures. Tom Meurer was always — and no doubt still is — promising his wife, Elaine, that in "ninety days" he would no longer "need to travel," a myth useful at the time.

After long periods of time away, it was considered by the Company appropriate to stay home a few weekdays to be with one's family. It probably occurred less often than many of us imagined it did since there were always new projects and crises that demanded attention.

I believe most of us exhibited a better than average record of attendance at our children's school plays, musicals, parent-teacher conferences and the like. We appreciated these events as once-in-a-lifetime occurrences and planned our business schedules, with definite support from the Company, to accommodate them. In my recollection, the office was virtually empty on Sundays.

Professional, Not Social Relationships

Bob Goldman or John Cullinane and I would play golf infrequently, and the Meurers socialized with the McKinneys, whom they had known back in Ohio, but there was limited socializing among employees. A few romantic attachments undoubtedly occurred but were conducted discreetly.

The fact that family values were acknowledged did not imply that exercise of them took place as part of an extended Cullinane Corporation "family." In the early years, there was only single function where spouses and companions were invited — the annual party at John Cullinane's house. By the mid-70s it was replaced by an annual Christmas dinner. As we grew, soft-ball games were instituted in the warmer weather and these kinds of group activities increased.

No one was afraid to "be wrong."

The atmosphere at Cullinane engendered a constant ebb and flow of discussion that was truly substantive — better ways to implement new features, ideas for wholly new products, clearer ways for customers to understand and use the software we were providing.

As a function of our small size, many of us were comfortable contributing across a range of areas that, in a larger organization, might be considered too broad. Accredited backgrounds in computer science and information management carried no particular weight, especially in brainstorming sessions. What counted were insight, understanding and the ability to exchange ideas with vigor.

Mutual Respect and Trust

The unusual atmosphere the Company fostered during its high-growth pre-public era — people working hard on shared goals — is shared by many small companies during comparable size and growth phases. Others, such as the willingness to eliminate dead wood quickly and the Company's high esteem for family life were, perhaps, more singular to our particular group of people at that time.

As the Company's size doubled and redoubled and eventually went public, some things were bound to change. Each of us took on a more specialized role, the usual raft of dread "policies and procedures" floated in and institutionalization inevitably crept in. It was largely unavoidable, an important step in the maturation of the organization. At the same time, though, many of the most important aspects of the unique Company culture persisted. The Company was "special," in large part because the people it comprised thought of themselves and of the organization that way. It was a good place to be.

A Personal View: Tom Meurer

In 1971, I worked as Database Administrator at the General Tire and Rubber Company in Akron, Ohio, one of the earliest installations of the TOTAL database management system. My staff and I had developed a report writer for TOTAL and for sequential files, and it worked well enough — or so we thought.

One day, the only salesman from a company I had not heard of visited General Tire to pitch a product called Culprit, which generated reports. I told him we had developed our own but would like to benchmark ours against his — to see how good a job we had done. The salesman went off to check with one "John Cullinane" and called me back to ask, "If Culprit proves superior to yours, will you buy it?" I said that sounded fair. Our system read and reported on a large tape file in one hour. Culprit did it in seven minutes. Who were these guys?

In a follow-up conversation with John Cullinane, I proposed an exchange. We would rewrite our interface to TOTAL so that Culprit could read TOTAL files, and he could then sell it to TOTAL users; he would provide General Tire with a license to use Culprit. He agreed and promptly sold the first copy of the interface to the Ford Motor Company. Then he asked if I would join his company, install the system at Ford and train their people.

Before accepting, I flew to Boston to meet John Cullinane and to have a long talk with him. The opportunity looked excellent, even though I was a little worried that there were only five people in the Company. I figured that the worse-case scenario would be that the job would not work out but by that time I would have had an inside look at many different companies where I would have installed software and trained people and, therefore, a broad base of knowledge and contacts to use in finding the next best job available. It looked like a win-win situation to me. I had no idea where it would lead, but it did have more opportunity and challenges than were available to me at General Tire. To my wife's horror, I accepted the job on May 1, 1972 and immediately began to travel four to five days per week. What I didn't learn at the start was that the Company had lost money for twelve of the thirteen previous months and was nearly out of cash — I had never thought to ask!

Operating with a Mentor and Lots of Freedom

John Cullinane gave me as much responsibility and involvement as I could handle. The rules were simple. Every move we made cost something, and you could see what it cost; so, make every move worthwhile. If I went on a sales call, I was to bring back either the business or a good reason why not. If I installed the system and trained the customer's staff, I was to stay until they were satisfied. If I were developing a new routine for Culprit in response to some customer's need, I was to deliver it on time and make sure it worked. This was dramatically different from the situation in a big company, where I often had no clue how the cost benefit of what I did affected my company's mission.

Each task was manageable and visible, and the results were easily measured. Whenever I fouled something up, John saw it, reviewed it with me and showed me where I had erred and what I could have done differently. This was always done in such a constructive way that I never went away upset, only determined to do better next time. It was his style.

Taking Corporate Risks

In early 1973, ownership rights to IDMS, a database management system, were up for grabs. John Cullinane, Jim Baker and I reviewed IDMS. Jim knew IMS and I knew TOTAL, and we concluded that IDMS was considerably better than both. Further, we knew we we could make it even better. The investment we would have to make would be in development support and sales activities. John Cullinane took a deep breath and truly bet the whole company on acquiring it. Simply put, if we weren't able to generate revenue reasonably quickly with IDMS, the Company would have gone bankrupt. Jim Baker was put in charge of Culprit, and I was handed IDMS.

From day one, I was buried in several hundred thousand lines of code I had never seen, facing customers in production whom I had never met. With John's encouragement, I hired Ron McKinney, Bill Casey and Bob Goldman. We were not managers, we were technicians, problem solvers and expediters. We listened to our prospects' needs and either explained how IDMS could meet their needs or expanded it in a way to meet a new need. We didn't know any other way to do business.

Through those first years, John Cullinane provided all the business sense and encouragement while we developed and delivered the goods. Gradually, we grew in business understanding and capability.

We needed additional staff, but we had no organization chart with boxes and responsibilities. We looked for people with a broad range of skills who were willing to do whatever it took to get the job done. We told people in interviews that from time to time they might be installing, teaching, selling, writing code or consulting, etc. We were so proud of our product, our company and our customers that we wanted to add only people that had the same capabilities and values we did.

Those who had the skills and were willing to do any of these things were introduced to John Cullinane, who would explain where he saw the Company going, the risks involved, his high standards and his business ethics. In almost every case, the prospect came out of his office ready to start work the next day.

Nines always attract other nines. There is no better example of the CEO (John Cullinane) hiring nines and those people in turn attracting more nines than the lineup that Cullinane Corporation fielded in the middle and late 1970s.

Who passed the screen in those early years? Tom Nelson from American Mutual, Nick Rini from Warner and Swazey, Don Heitzmann from Rhode Island Hospital, Dave Ireland from Bache Securities, Bill Linn from Southern Railway, Joe Demartino, a consultant to U.S. Surgical, Andrew Filipowski from A. B. Dick, Ray Nawara from Cook County Hospital, Brock Shaw from Univac, Bob Davis from Cincom, Frank Chisholm from Scott Paper, and many more. Jon Nackerud was already managing the West Coast operations. This team always had the customer's needs foremost in mind and regularly beat the competition (IBM and Cincom), which had larger staffs and better financing. Through the 1970s, the sales and profits nearly doubled every year.

In my mind, I had to find out if I could make it on my own, and I left the Company to start my own venture. John listened to my plan and gave me the same encouragement and advice that he had always given: Listen closely to the customer, and do what he asks. Hire only nines; tell them what needs to be done and, as long as they are doing it, stay out of their way. Treat people really well, both financially and as human beings. Keep high ethical standards, especially during the difficult times. And, finally, seek advice; then, use good judgment.

When I have followed John's advice, the results have always been good. When things appear to have turned bad, a review of these principles puts me back on the right track.

MY VIEW

In 1977, a year before we went public, a key vice president asked me the following question, "What is it that you do, anyhow?" I was stunned. I thought that he, of all people, understood that our great success didn't happen by accident and that he appreciated that I was ultimately responsible for it by keeping all the balls in the air, producing the Company's outstanding financial results and pushing the Company into new technological areas.

Obviously, he, and undoubtedly others, didn't share this view. What was ironic was that I was in the process of making them multimillionaires. I think the secret was that most of our key people felt that they were responsible for the Company's success, which to a significant degree, they were and also that I was often doing things that, perhaps, the value of which they did not understand at the time.

A typical example around the time of this comment was when I negotiated the 1977 television sponsorship of the United States Pro Tennis Championship at Longwood Cricket Club (Brookline, Mass.). Along with three major corporations, including American Airlines, the Company would cosponsor the semifinals of the Tournament, which was shown across America on the Public Broadcasting System. On Monday night, the Company would have exclusive sponsorship in Massachusetts for a total cost of $25,000. I thought this was quite a coup. However, when I announced it, my staff questioned the decision. "Why are we doing it?" they asked.

I knew that the Company would be going public within a year and the name, "Cullinane Corporation," would become instantly known to a lot of tennis players who were also investment bankers or worked for financial institutions across the Country. By their nature, they would be curious about a company they had never heard of, which was exactly what happened.

This little episode illustrates the relationship between me and the Company's vice presidents. They were mostly technicians and (with the exception of Jon Nackerud) much younger than I. Controlling such a bright and opinionated group could be a challenge at times, but we did have a lot of laughs. They reveled in the camaraderie and the technical challenges of developing, installing, supporting and selling the products with their contemporaries.

A company is a business, not a religion.

Humor was where you found it. For example, on my rare trips to the west coast, Jon Nackerud often introduced me to prospects and clients by telling them that, when the Company was founded, it was named the Cullinane Corporation. Then they had to go looking for a president, and I was the first one named Cullinane they found.

As president, a nontechnician and a member of a different generation but with a nonduplicative set of interests and skills in management, marketing, etc., it was natural that I could not be a member of this group. More importantly, we had a company that was good technically but also knew how to sell and make money, an unusual combination in the software business.

It wasn't until many of these individuals founded their own companies that I heard, "Now I know what you were talking about." Nevertheless, what I did know from the beginning was how outstanding so many of these individuals were. I used to tell them every so often that because of them the Company was the best software company in the world. At first I don't think they believed me, but in time, they learned that it was true.

In 1976, I remember saying to Jim Baker, "Remember these times because they are the halcyon days." Actually, they lasted years longer than I had expected. I would like to say it was a lot of fun for me while it lasted, but it wasn't. It was a lot of work and a lot of worry, and there's not a lot of camaraderie when you're the president.

In many ways, we took for granted what we did. There was a right way to do something, not a "Cullinane" way, and we tried to do it that way. A lot of praise for doing a good job was viewed with suspicion. However, there were moments of great pride in the Company and User Weeks never failed to generate that feeling. I used to walk by the training classes in the morning and be awed by the number of them and how each class was full of users. With hundreds of courses underway located over a number of hotels serving thousands of users, I couldn't help but think of how far the Company had come since it was founded.

However, I always thought of the Company as a business and not a religion. Its purpose was to make money by satisfying customer requirements, and this it did better than any other software company for many years. Finally, I tried not to succumb to the accoutrements of great corporate success, such as personal jets, corporate campuses, personal public relations, etc. Consequently, if the inevitable crash happened, I wouldn't have too far to fall. As a result, getting off the "power base" hasn't been too difficult an experience. In fact, life gets more enjoyable all the time.

INTEGRITY IN BUSINESS

When I formed the Company, I suspected that I would probably have to cut corners to succeed; didn't everyone in business? However, I made a commitment to myself that, if I had to sacrifice my sense of ethics to succeed, I wasn't going to do it. If this meant failure, so be it. I suspect that it's my parochial school education that has left me with a conscience that I have to live with for life. Then, again, maybe it was my upbringing. Nevertheless, I was most pleasantly surprised to discover that integrity in business was not a burden but, rather, a great asset.

It's also nice to know that I am not unique in this experience. At a conference of very successful entrepreneurs held at the Harvard Business School, integrity was cited as a key competitive factor in their respective companies' successes.

I mention this because some have wondered whether the Company was unique in this regard. I even had the president of a business school express his appreciation of my stressing integrity to his student body because some of his professors taught that it may be necessary to cut corners to succeed. I was shocked to hear this.

Integrity in business

is a great asset, not a burden.

When I think of my experiences in corporate America, many companies seem to fall into one of two categories. They either operate with integrity or are corporate zoos. The good firms bring out the best in people; the zoos bring out the worst. In fact, most people can't cope with the zoos because they don't have a devious or paranoiac way of thinking.

When I think of the places that I have worked, marvelous companies like Arthur D. Little, Inc. come to mind. John Hanly, my first boss, was tough, fair and honest. He was always a role model. George White at CEIR, with Alan Shoolman's support, gave me my first promotion when it would have been very easy not to and I would never have known. Isaac Auerbach and Arnie Shafritz at Auerbach Corporation were first-class people; so were the people at Phillip Hankins & Co. However, whenever I was involved in a corporate-zoo situation, I just did what I thought was right, and it always seemed to work out in the long run. That doesn't mean that it was any fun at the time.

By the way, be a little wary of people who wear their integrity on their sleeves.

POSITIVE VS. NEGATIVE SOLUTIONS

People in business do have conflicts, like everyone else. The important question is, What do you do when you have a conflict? When there is a disagreement, you really have only two choices: a positive solution or a negative one. With a positive solution, you try to find an arrangement that benefits both parties; with a negative solution, you hire a lawyer and go to court. Always seek out a positive solution — never go to court if you can possibly help it.

The Company never had a lawsuit with a client during 20 years in an extraordinarily complex business. We did have one with another vendor, and it wasn't a very enjoyable experience. It only confirmed the wisdom of bending over backwards to avoid any lawsuit.

Always look for

positive solutions to problems.

Key employees that may not be working out for legitimate reasons are another example. On a number of occasions, I encouraged these employees to form their own companies and helped them get started with funding or business. It was a perfect and positive solution that benefited both parties.

BELLES OF THE BALL

On one occasion when I was badgering my wife to attend the Company's User Group Meeting, she said, "Why don't you take your mother, since the plane ticket says Mrs. Cullinane and there are two Mrs. Cullinanes." I agreed and suggested her mother come along to keep my mother company. However, I wondered how I would find the time to look after them and thousands of users at the same time.

Well, they were no problem at all. Employees and customers were fascinated by them because they were full of life and humor. They were the "belles of the ball." They were asked by users to dance, and you could see the years fall away as they became young girls again.

From then on, it became a tradition for them to attend User Weeks as long as my mother was physically able. We would assign them the Presidential Suite, which we would get free, or whatever the most elaborate suite was at some elegant resort, such as the Boca Raton Hotel and Club. Once I showed them how to call room service, they were all set. They would also receive VIP treatment from all the hotel's staff. Invited speakers, such as Art Buchwald, would treat them royally. User Week, I believe, was one of the most exciting things that ever happened to them. My mother playing Black Jack for the first time in her life with Mrs. Haverty, my wife's mother, in a Las Vegas casino was an unforgettable experience. I am sure the casino people assigned to watch things from above the floor wondered who they were.

They're never too old to be young again.

Many of the people attending made the gesture of telling me how nice it was to have brought them. Yet, I knew I was receiving the true satisfaction of watching them have a new lease on life. I think they also helped the image of parents and grandparents because we saw more of them in attendance at subsequent User Weeks.

WHAT DRIVES PEOPLE

Money is not really the most important driving force for people. Recognition and appreciation by their peers drive people. Why else would some captain of industry work long hours to raise money for a charity in order to exceed the previous year's amount? He or she wants the respect of those people involved, a recognition that he or she can do a better job than their predecessors. When an individual's personal name is on the line, it is amazing how hard he or she will work to accomplish the goal.

When the Company went public in 1978, a number of relatively young people became millionaires. This was the moment for which they had been waiting; now they could have a bigger house, an expensive car, boat or whatever they had wanted for so long. I am sure that many of them felt as most of us do, "If I only had a million dollars, I would be happy."

> *Respect and appreciation*
>
> *for what they do are the*
>
> *driving forces for most people.*

But if you were to speak with them afterwards, you would have found that once they had the money, the bigger car, house, etc., it hadn't changed their lives very much, and it hadn't made them any happier. In some cases, this feeling puzzled them. In the final analysis, people still like to be appreciated for what they do.

Management's challenge is to honor that need and to help create an environment where people can not only succeed but be recognized for it by others who have the same high standards and values.

NEW IDEAS

New ideas are the lifeblood of a company, and the goal of senior managers ought to be to create an atmosphere where good ideas can flourish. Good ideas can come from a variety of sources within a company, and it is very important to remember who was responsible for the idea.

If ideas begin to be appropriated without recognition, the flow of innovation will stop because people shut down when they are around idea-takers. It is easy to forget where ideas originate, however. It can happen to anyone. For example, whenever I was at a cocktail party during the 1970s, people would often ask, "What business are you in?" I would say, "the software products business," and you could see their eyes glaze over. No effort of explaining seemed to remove that glaze. So, I thought of a player piano analogy, whereby the player piano was the hardware and the software was the roll that made the computer play its "tune," and people understood this analogy immediately. I used it many time times, including on Wall Street, when I had to explain the software business so often because we were the first software products company to go public. It became a widely used metaphor.

It's easy to forget whose idea it was.

Once, Cable News Network ran a week-long series on software and asked me to participate. I planned to use the player piano analogy to kick off my interview. CNN wired me up in New York and I was waiting for the countdown for my interview, which would come from Atlanta. Before they cut to me, they reviewed the interview with John Imlay, Chairman of Management Sciences America, a major software company and competitor, that had taken place the previous day. I noticed he had used "my" player piano analogy. I almost panicked. I couldn't believe it. I had ten seconds before I had to go on the air. Fortunately, I came up with a new analogy fast. The interview went very well, but it was a very tense moment for me.

Some time later, I was speaking with my sister, *Mary, who was always interested in the Company, about how I felt when my idea had been used and how unfair it was, because the competitor had to have known that I had used it many times before. My sister startled me by saying, "The player piano analogy wasn't your idea. It was mine; I told it to you a long time ago." The more I thought about it, the more I realized she was right. I was embarrassed.

The point is that ideas can come from anywhere, and there's a great tendency to forget where they originated. A manager should bend over backwards to acknowledge the source of ideas. It will encourage innovation, and it will avoid the problem of people shutting down because they feel others are taking advantage of their insight.

Mary Eidson: Mary and her husband, Bill Eidson, were always intensely interested in the Company. Bill, an expert in advertising, served on the Board of Directors for many years and was extremely helpful with our advertising. I must say I was the bane of his and other advertising people's existence for my headstrong approach to the subject. In defense, I was meeting with customers and prospects daily and knew what worked.

COMPETITION

There is a great tendency on the part of any company's sales force to either view the competition as larger than life or to denigrate it. Both approaches are mistakes. A company should never view the competition as invincible, nor should a company use "negative campaigning."

If you have anything to say

about a competitor, make it positive.

One of the Company's competitors was continually spreading some negative story or another about the Company to mutual prospects. I solved this problem by confronting him at an industry conference and promising that I would use all Company resources to win any business when the Company was in competition with the competitor for a contract. In other words, I let him know his tactics were going to cost him a lot of business in an environment where there were more opportunities than resources available to pursue them. He got the message.

One of the Company's marketing rules was not to knock competition. If anything was said, the sales force was to make sure it was positive. I learned the benefit of this on my first sales call many years before. I knocked a competitor and the prospect immediately leapt to the competitor's defense. It didn't feel good knocking the competition; it also didn't work.

In a subsequent meeting, I made sure to praise the competitor. I was surprised to hear the prospect respond by quickly listing the competitor's deficiencies. I never forgot this experience.

Competition with IBM's IMS database management system became much easier for the Company when we conceded that it was a very powerful database management system. The major difference between the Company's IDMS and IBM's IMS was that IDMS was dictionary-driven and IMS wasn't. This was a fact, not some subjective opinion. The next step in our sales pitch was to prove why there were many advantages to a dictionary-driven database management system, in terms that prospects and buyers, including management, could understand.

THE TEN CHARACTERISTICS OF
A GOOD COMPANY WITH A GOOD CULTURE

Good companies

are easy to do business with.

1. When you call, the phone is answered within three rings.

2. If the person answering the phone can't help you, he or she knows who can and makes an effort to connect you.

3. The right person answers your question and generates further interest on your part in the company's products or services and, if possible, closes the business.

4. The company is easy to do business with; it has no artificial barriers to consummating a sale, such as complicated agreements.

5. Employees enjoy working for the company, and it shows in their good humor and camaraderie. As a result, there is little turnover.

6. The company is a leader in innovation related to social issues of the day.

7. If there is a problem with the product or service, the company doesn't argue with you but, rather, acknowledges the problem and does something about it.

8. The company anticipates your requirements. New products and services reflect your needs without your having to ask for them.

9. The company goes the extra mile in service and gives you something that you never expected to get.

10. The company makes money.

Chapter Ten

Personal Points

RESPONSIBILITIES OF
THE SUCCESSFUL ENTREPRENEUR

It's easy for a successful entrepreneur to get a big head. You've made a lot of money, people are in awe of you, and they listen carefully when you speak the "new truth." You have the "right stuff," and you're a "master of the universe" for at least as long as the stock is climbing. It's easy to get a little puffy and say that, if other people only worked as hard as you did, they would be successful, too.

The truth is that very few people in business, if any, ever made it completely on their own. In my case, my sister Teresa and her husband, Frank Vaughan, "lent" me their total savings to continue in school.

While working hard is a necessary element of success, it isn't sufficient. Anyone who has done well in life has more than likely had a lot of help, a lot more than he or she may be willing to acknowledge, or remember for that matter. In many cases, the help might have come from family and friends, but in other cases the government or a community program may have provided assistance. And there was often a person who happened to be there at the right time and with the right advice. What would have happened if that weren't the case? I have often thought about this and how many people helped me along the way and how many people don't get that help when they really need it.

One thing that has always puzzled me about some very successful entrepreneurs is their unwillingness to give away large amounts of stock to various charities, including their respective schools. I suspect that they never thought about it too much.

Let's assume that entrepreneur X's company has gone public, and it's a raving success. A few stock splits later, and X has salted away a cool $100 million and has $400 million left in company stock, which is very difficult to sell because of Rule 144 of the SEC. In other words, our entrepreneur can sell only relatively few shares every quarter and be identified as a selling insider. The great danger is that, in time, the company will have some bad times, as all companies have, and the $400 million in company stock could shrink to as little as $40 million.

We assume that our entrepreneur has long since diversified the $100 million; so, it isn't impacted by this drop in the company's stock. Thus, it would have been much better if the entrepreneur had given away a big chunk of his or her stock when it was selling at its high. To do otherwise is to run the real risk of "burning" $360 million when it could have done a lot of good for a lot of people. What I find ironic is that the stock is essentially "paper" to the entrepreneur but real gold to the recipients because they can sell it immediately.

> *An entrepreneur has an obligation*
>
> *to give something back.*

If you have been successful, you owe it to others to help them realize their potential. This requires that organizations be good corporate citizens and do everything they can to help improve society and create opportunities for others.

It's a form of enlightened self-interest for business leaders to put something back into the society that helped them become who they are. What's good for America is good for your company and, better still, for your children and their future. Otherwise, you will have to build walls around your house to keep the less fortunate out, which is certainly happening in America.

POLITICS & BUSINESS

In 1981, at the suggestion of Breen Murray of Breen Murray Securities, Inc., I joined a new group called the American Business Conference (ABC), comprised of 100 of the fastest growing companies in America with sales under 200 million dollars. The Chairman of ABC was Arthur Leavitt, at the time President of the American Stock Exchange. ABC's President was Jack Albertine, an economist who was highly regarded around Washington and, in particular, the White House.

President Reagan was particularly responsive to self-made men and women and this type of group, as were key members of his staff. Consequently, we were invited to meet with him personally at the White House on two occasions.

> *Large companies' interests*
>
> *are not the same*
>
> *as small companies' interests.*

A lot of decisions entrepreneurs make are determined by whom one has decided to believe. For example, during one ABC session in March 1981, President Reagan's Cabinet appointees said the deficit wasn't going to exceed $30 million, but Senator Ernest Hollings of South Carolina, in his inimitable style, thought it was going to exceed $100 billion. Which one was I to believe? The more I thought about it, the more I was inclined toward Senator Hollings' position. I went back to Boston with the distinct feeling that the next couple of years would be very difficult. Consequently, I implemented a cost-cutting program, combined with aggressive new product introductions. As a result of moving fast, the Company continued to grow at the 50 per cent rate in sales and profits during the period of 1981-1983, while other companies fell on hard times because this period was close to a depression for many.

Large companies' interests were not always the same as small companies' interests – one of the surprising things I learned from ABC meetings. For example, some of the largest American companies pay no taxes. The result is that, while large companies may generate 35 per cent of the sales of the United States' economy, they pay only about 23 per cent of the taxes. Companies such as those represented at the ABC were paying the reverse – 35 per cent of corporate taxes, while generating 23 per cent of sales.

POLITICS & BUSINESS, Continued ...

One year, President Reagan's staff inserted, at the last minute, a paragraph about high technology being the "savior" of America in his State of the Union Speech. As a follow-up, some of his staff suggested the President visit Boston and its Route 128 high-tech companies, featuring a stop at Digital Equipment Corporation's headquarters in Maynard as a related public relations effort.

However, I suspect both Jack Albertine and Dee d'Arbeloff, Chairman of the Board of Millipore Corporation and a key player in the American Business Conference and the Massachusetts High Technology Council, recognized an opportunity. Jack, working with the White House staff, got the meeting agenda changed from a visit to Digital's headquarters to a visit to Boston and the Millipore facility.

The main feature of the stop at Millipore was a panel made up of members of the Massachusetts High Technology Council asking questions of the President in a televised forum with hundreds of high-tech CEOs in attendance. I was asked to be on the panel and agreed to ask a question assigned to me. In fact, all panel members accepted the condition since, we were told, questions had to be approved by the White House in advance.

We all met at Millipore headquarters the evening before to rehearse – it was, indeed, staged in every way. The question assigned to me was on the President's plans for education, which he had mentioned in his State of the Union speech.

The big day arrived, and we, as well as the high-tech CEOs in the audience, had to be at Millipore's headquarters hours in advance of the President's arrival. The time of the President's arrival came and went. Finally, Dee d'Arbeloff, perhaps thinking that I, being of Irish descent, would be pleased, told me that the Presidential motorcade had stopped at the Eire Pub in Dorchester. However, I wasn't too enthusiastic about the President publicly stereotyping the Irish as drinkers.

The net result was that the President was two hours late for the visit to Millipore, a bonus in a way in that it gave me the opportunity to converse with the person seated to my right, Chuck McKay, Executive Vice President of the Foxboro Company. Originally from South Carolina and extremely conservative in his political views, Chuck seemed to have a political perspective irreconcilably different from mine; however, once we got off party lines and started discussing social issues, we found we were in remarkable agreement. We discussed the causes of a long list of problems and their solutions. Had we not been sitting beside each other for two hours, we might never have explored each other's positions to sufficient depth to reconcile them.

Typecasting does everyone a disservice.

President Reagan was very pleasant although, I believe, a bit wary and uncomfortable about being in front of such a high-powered, high-tech audience. He needn't have worried, but I am sure he was somewhat apprehensive that members of the group were going to ask him some very tough questions. In fact, when I asked him the question about education, he became uncomfortable as he didn't have any real answers. I felt like protesting, "Don't blame me; it's not my question!" but he then told some humorous anecdote, and that was it.

By the way, the big coverage on television and in the newspapers was of the President's stop at the Eire Pub, not what went on at Millipore.

WOMEN AT WORK

Some women are single parents and have to work to survive; other women have to work to maintain a reasonable standard of living; still other women work because they want to. In each case, the woman has to cope with two jobs, work and home. Women certainly don't have it easy. Compounding the problem is that women have really been taken advantage of in the work place for years. For example, my mother-in-law was a nurse and the working hours, tasks and conditions that nurses were subjected to is unbelievable by today's standards. The doctor was, and is, king and gets all the money, while the nurse does all the work. Likewise, secretaries work extremely hard, have to be at their desks all the time, make critical decisions, are often asked for their advice and are poorly paid. Like the nurses of my mother-in-law's era, "That's the way it is." It shouldn't be.

Women sure don't have it easy.

Things really get complicated and emotional when children enter the picture. One poignant example was told to me recently by my driver on the way to the airport who had just taken a former vice president of the Company to the airport. As she left the house, her child was crying uncontrollably. She was torn between wanting to stay and find out what was wrong with her child and catching the airplane to some meeting, probably with an important client or prospect, where her presence was critical. What a decision for any mother to have to make.

Another example is when the Company's Chief Financial Officer had a child by Caesarean operation after having recently adopted two children. Phyllis Swersky now had three children under two years of age at a time when it was a high tension period in the Company's history, and she had just come from a highly emotional and very difficult operation. I don't know what the answer is, but juggling two careers is not easy. Fortunately, in Phyllis Swersky's case, her spouse, Jeff, was, and is, very supportive.

The issue of day care is, I believe, enormously important. I think companies could be much more flexible and imaginative in this area than they are. For example, I think that women should be able to bring their children to work, if possible, rather than leaving them at a day care center. I realize that this will introduce some problems, but they can be worked out. I just think that the more time a child spends with its mother, particularly at a young age, the better.

However, there is nothing in business that women can't do well. Many women, through experience, are gaining the necessary confidence and, thanks to equal opportunity legislation, they are receiving equal pay. However, to repeat, women sure don't have it easy.

INVESTMENT STRATEGY

Steve McClellan, software industry analyst for Merrill Lynch (New York and Los Angeles) recently asked a group of software company CEOs at a Boston conference that I attended whether software companies are boom and bust investments. While there may be some exceptions to this phenomenon, there are not many.

Establish an investment life

for a software company.

As background, the software industry is primarily a niche business. It is very easy to enter, and new participants have a built-in advantage over established competitors because they don't have an existing customer base to worry about and convert to the new technology. Also, software is better developed by a smart, lean and hungry group. Many software company CEOs, however, have little management experience, particularly coping with growth. In addition, as a company grows dramatically, it has difficulty maintaining the growth in its niche.

My advice to investors is to participate in the IPOs and establish an "investment life" for the company. This may be one day, one year, three years, etc. When that period is up, take your profits and don't look back. History shows that too many software companies hit brick walls to do otherwise.

"LOOK & FEEL"

One of the hot legal issues today is the "look and feel" of software. In other words, how close is a new product to the product with which it was designed to compete? This, of course, is more difficult than the issue of stealing someone else's code. There is inherent danger in the "look and feel" issue, though: It has a great potential to inhibit the development of software. One of the problems is that every software product is an evolution of another product. Most software has something to do with one of three activities: getting data into a computer, maintaining it or presenting it. The rest has to do with housekeeping activities necessary to run a computer.

A related "look and feel" incident involving a major computer vendor illustrates the potential problem. It took place when a senior executive of the vendor called me out of the blue to inform me that the Company's new telecommunications monitor, IDMS-DC, had infringed on the copyright of their telecommunications monitor. The executive wanted to visit us and bring the vendor's lawyer and industry representative. I told the executive that, knowing the IDMS-DC development staff involved, I didn't think this was the case. But I told them to come ahead if they wanted to, and come they did.

The executive had an overhead viewgraph presentation prepared by a consultant who had reviewed IDMS-DC manuals. In the course of the presentation, the executive made it clear that the Company was guilty.

When the executive finished, I said that one of the nice things about the Company was that key people stayed with the Company. In fact, the developers of IDMS-DC were still part of our development group. They included *Don Heitzmann, Nick Rini and David Litwack.

I called Don and asked him to come to the Company's Board room right away. When he arrived, I asked the executive to make the presentation again. Don then proceeded to completely blow the executive out of the water.

One of the executive's points was that we named certain control blocks with initials similar to theirs. Don pointed out that they were his initials, not the vendor's. Don did a fantastic job on every point. But rather than apologizing, the executive insisted on sending two systems programmers, much to the embarrassment of the executive's associates, to actually look at the code of IDMS-DC, line by line. I agreed to let them do this, and they found nothing.

> ## *"Look and feel" lawsuits*
> ## *will inhibit software development.*

However, they couldn't understand how we could have developed a new version of IDMS-DC without having gotten our hands on proprietary information. The answer was simple: Their company had provided us with the appropriate manual necessary to interface IDMS-DC with their protocols. They were astonished to see a copy of the manual because they didn't know it existed. The final score was the Company 1,000, the vendor 0.

I don't think I was ever prouder of the Company than I was after this experience. Doing business with integrity has a way of paying off in so many unanticipated ways. However, the "look and feel" message in this experience is that a large company, simply because it has the legal resources and money, can put a small company on the defensive with this issue.

In reading business plans for new software companies, it becomes obvious that the "look and feel" issue is becoming of great importance. One business plan spent a major portion on the lawsuits or potential lawsuits over this issue.

Don Heitzmann: Don came from Rhode Island Hospital, where he had been an outstanding systems programmer. He, along with David Litwack and Nick Rini, developed IDMS-DC, the only teleprocessing monitor that I know of developed for IBM computers in the last 20 years. They did it in two years, and it was a great success. They designed it the same time as a new version of IDMS and the Integrated Data Dictionary were being designed. The result was a terrific system that would allow the changing of networks within minutes.

POWER BASE

The most difficult experience for any executive is to learn to cope with is the loss of his or her power base. The reason is that most executives eventually forget that it is the position that gives them the power. Learning otherwise after it is too late can come as a shock. Compounding the problem is the number and quality of the "perks" that one had become accustomed to, including corporate jets, invitations to prestigious golf tournaments, chairmanships of major fund raising or social events and boards of directors. To lose access to all of these accoutrements of power and influence, literally overnight in some cases, is a bitter pill to swallow. What better example is there than the President of the United States. Once his eight years (or four years) have been completed, what does he do?

When corporate America is over for you, and it eventually will be, what are you going to do next? The reason that this question is so important is that many former CEOs, regardless of their success history, don't have than many attractive options. For example, they can become CEO of a competing company, president of a university, head of a foundation, start a new venture, play golf, sit around and drive their wives crazy learning to play the piano as I did for a couple of weeks. None of the above, in my opinion, is very exciting because we have done so much of it before.

While I work just as hard as ever, my life style is very different than it once was. Instead of spending 80% of my time doing what others want or expect of me, I spend 80% of my time doing what I want to do and — most important — when I want to do it. For example, if it is a beautiful day, I will literally go fishing and then play golf. If the weather is bad, I work. However, what I have not been able to do is come up with a satisfactory one-sentence answer to the question I often hear at a cocktail party, "What are you doing now?"

I have an extremely busy and varied schedule of important activities that can't be reduced to venture capital, management consulting, investments, sailing around the world, etc. All I know is what I am doing is a lot more enjoyable than worrying about whether the Company is going to meet its numbers for the thirtieth quarter in a row. However, it took about a year for this metamorphosis to take place.

Power comes from the position.

While building a company from an idea to very successful venture is a very satisfying experience, the very success becomes a trap with no easy way out. Continued success demands even more success. It also requires solving the same problems over and over again. What's particularly ironic is that the more successful a company becomes, the more management structure in place, the more boring are the issues that end up on the president's desk.

HONORS

During the years 1968 to 1978, I received no recognition or honors. However, once the Company went public and became highly visible, particularly as the stock split four times, I became the recipient of an increasing number of honors. Once the Company's stock price dropped, though, the awards slowed down. Ironically, once the Company became well known, I didn't need any recognition; when it was unknown, I could have used some. For example, I most appreciated the first article about the Company by Ron Rosenberg of *The Boston Globe* entitled "Quite Simply, a Big Success." [Globe]

Most of these honors, I eventually came to realize, bore some relation or another to fund raising, albeit for a worthy cause, and I was expected to sell a lot of tables for the event. One notable exception was the time that Northeastern University wanted to name a building after me. I declined but suggested, "Why not name it after my parents, David and Margaret Cullinane?"

> *Beware of fund raisers bearing honors.*

My mother, with her soft Irish accent, was a big hit when, from her wheelchair, she spoke to a crowd for the first time in her life. At the last minute, I asked Northeastern to insert the name of Fitzgerald in honor of my mother's brother who was 92 years old and a great family favorite. Unfortunately, he had been in a nursing home for the past year because of a stroke. As a result, he couldn't speak, which was a tragedy because he was such a good story teller. He loved to follow the Company and kept a notebook on it. When my sister told him that his name was to be included on the building of Northeastern's new College of Computer Science, he smiled. He died that night.

[Globe]   Ron Rosenberg, "Quite Simply, a Big Success," *The Boston Globe*, September 30, 1980.

SPOUSES

When I was thinking about forming a new company, it was my wife who took the pressure off the decision. This was key. In other words, she made it clear that if the venture failed, it wasn't the end of the world, we could do something else, including both of us getting a job if necessary. I can't tell you how important the removal of this pressure was in my decision to form a company. As a result, I wasn't afraid to fail.

Previously, she had encouraged me to leave a job if I were not happy with it, regardless of how financially rewarding the job might or could be. In one case, it meant leaving a job when I owned a major equity position in a company that obviously was going to be worth a lot of money in the foreseeable future. It was her belief that my well-being was more important than any financial reward from the job, no matter how great.

> *Spouses, especially wives,*
>
> *rarely get any credit.*

Finally, it is so important to have someone sufficiently objective about a company with whom you can discuss ideas regarding new developments affecting the company or whose advice you can seek. In my case, my wife was this person. Her insight was always a great asset to me and the Company.

As the saying goes, I couldn't have done it without her.

WHY DID IT HAVE TO HAPPEN TO ME?

By 1981, the Company was humming on all cylinders. I felt we were strong in every important category   good products, good strategy, good management team under development and an enviable record in the industry and on Wall Street. Industry surveys showed the Company to be Number 1 in overall user satisfaction, documentation, training, support and performance.

So, by 1983, after continued good performance by the management team and a change in name, I felt it was time to move on. However, I continued as Chairman of the Board. Then, in 1985 came our first down quarter. It eventually would be as bad as my worst nightmare. After 13 years of great performance, just when I was about to leave, I asked myself, "Why did it have to happen to me?"

Around this time, I was invited to an Executive Day by Digital Equipment Corporation as part of their Annual Seniors Pro-Am Golf Tournament. The morning session was devoted to lectures by an economist and a former psychiatrist for the Harvard Business School by the name of Dr. Barry Greiff. Dr. Greiff gave a sparkling talk on a businessperson's responsibilities beyond the business, including the family.

As part of this session, he handed out a book that contained many experiences of other CEOs who also asked, "Why did it have to happen to me?" It dawned on me that these things happen to everyone, not just me. The reason that we are not so aware of events that happen to others is that we are not, by nature, anywhere nearly as interested in what is happening to others as we are to what is happening to ourselves. Conversely, we think others are as interested in us and our activities as we are.

It happens to everyone.

In reality, others don't care very much or at all about what we are doing. So, when an article appears in the newspaper that may be negative about us or our company, we read every word believing the type is in large, blinking neon lights. Someone else just skims over the article or doesn't notice it at all. It's no big deal to them. In fact, almost every time I mentioned to someone a negative article that had been published about the Company, they hadn't read it.

The more I thought about what happens to others and how difficult it must be for them, my "Why did it have to happen to me?" lament disappeared. I didn't worry about it anymore. Nobody else is that interested, why should I be? Besides, God never guaranteed me or anyone a free ride in this world. There are always ups and downs. They are easier to cope with when you take this perspective as opposed to personalizing it. It also helps if your family is behind you.

THE KEY IS THE FAMILY.

While everyone agrees that family is important, some people use work pressures as a cop-out. He or she will be away from home, traveling or working late, and tell their spouse, I'm doing it all for you," or "I'm doing it for the kids." But after months or years of this type of work habit, the spouse's response will be, "Yes, but what good is it?" Certainly, the family wants the economic benefits of a successful career but not at the expense of the family unit itself.

We should operate as if the children and their events are just as important as business events. For example, I found that it really worked to put my children's events on my calendar just like other important meetings. My secretary then built my meetings around those events, instead of my finding out at the last minute that my son or daughter had an important function that I couldn't attend. If your son has a baseball game, or your daughter is in a play, put that on the calendar and build your meetings around them and go to them. The world won't come to an end if you don't attend another business meeting. However, yours might if your children grow up so fast that you miss the whole experience.

> *Family is all we have*
>
> *in the final analysis.*

I was once in Brussels for a three-day user meeting that was well staffed and well organized. As I lay in bed early Friday morning, on the third day, I asked myself, "What am I doing here?" I knew that the meeting could get along very well without me, and my seventh-grade son had a football game at home that afternoon. Frankly, I was homesick so I said, "I'm going." I called Sabena and got the last seat on the 8:00 a.m. flight to London, which arrived in time for me to catch a TWA flight to Boston. I got there just in time for the opening kickoff.

It was a beautiful September day in a splendid setting. My son looked up out of the huddle and saw me. He gave me a quick little wave, which said that he missed me and was pleased to see me home safely. Normally, like most young athletes, he would never acknowledge his father while on the field of play, but he did this time. It had an emotional impact on me similar to the time my daughter Sue spontaneously ran into my arms as I exited Customs after a long trip and clutched me tightly.

Just being there for my daughter has its own rewards, and it meant a lot more to my son and me that I was at his game than it might have meant to the people in Brussels if I had stayed on for the rest of the meeting.

Working smart instead of working hard is the way to have a strong family life and a successful career at the same time. Regardless of what anyone tells you, it is not necessary to take work home at night if you don't want to do it. The truth is that some people really don't want to leave work at all. They get into a kind of "hyper-zone" that gives them an "up," and they simply do not want to come down from it.

Being busy all the time, keeping people waiting and taking telephone calls all give the appearance of being very important, and it can feel as if you are highly productive. As a rule, however, if you are overly busy, it means that you are going to too many meetings, traveling too often, and you are not setting priorities on how you spend your time.

Most meetings are a waste of time and 60% of all trips are not necessary because a telephone call would do the job. And remember that most telephone calls are also twice as long as they should be.

If you make your family a priority, you will be forced to work more efficiently. You'll get to the heart of the matter, putting issues on the table and resolving them. How many times have you had just five minutes to discuss something of great significance with an important client or member of management because, if you took any longer, you were going to miss your flight. Isn't it interesting, under these circumstances, how quickly you can get to the point and resolve the issue, if possible.

These types of comments may be disconcerting to many people. They would rather justify their work habits because they "have to." The point is that you don't have to.

Work smart, as well as hard.

Make family life a priority, and it will help you cope with, "Why did it have to happen to me?" when it happens to you — because it does happen to everybody, sooner or later.

I don't remember what was said in that meeting in Brussels, but I do remember my son's smile and wave on a beautiful day in September and how glad my daughter, Sue, was to see me.

Index

Also Available from BUSINESS ONE IRWIN:

THE SECRET EMPIRE
How 25 Multinationals Rule the World
Janet Lowe

Lowe identifies the leading multinationals, describing what they do, their corporate personalities and who runs them, and shows the impact multinationals have on shareholders, workers, consumers and governments.
ISBN: 1-55623-513-5

EXECUTIVE TALENT
How to Identify and Develop the Best
Tom Potts and Arnold Sykes

Cultivate and grow internal executive resources for succession planning and corporate growth! Shows how to realize the full potential of every employee in the organization.
ISBN: 1-55623-754-5

POWER VISION
How to Unlock the Six Dimensions of Executive Potential
George W. Watts

Achieve peak performance through self-assessment. Watts shows you how to become a more effective manager who makes profitable and positive contributions to your company.
ISBN: 1-55623-808-8

ON YOUR OWN
How to Start, Develop and Manage a New Business
Robert D. Hisrich and Michael P. Peters

Eliminates the guesswork in starting and growing a new venture by giving you a one-step source outlining all the vital information you will need for success. Includes valuable worksheets, checklists and forms to save you time and money.
ISBN: 1-55623-650-6

MAVERICKS!
How to Lead Your Staff to Think like Einstein, Create like da Vinci and Invent like Edison
Donald W. Blohowiak

Liberate the boundless energy and creativity of your employees for more innovative, profitable ideas. You'll discover that you can encourage reluctant workers to get the most out of their jobs by giving more of themselves, build teamwork by treating everyone as a unique individual and inspire loyalty by granting independence.
ISBN: 1-55623-624-7

Available at fine bookstores and libraries everywhere.